ABOUT THE AUTHOR

Dan Albaum is an accomplished marketing leader with experience launching new products and driving world-class results in global technology companies including Verizon Wireless, Cisco, Honeywell, Consumer Packaged Goods (CPG), and the non-profit space. He is a passionate servant leader empowering teams to create stronger internal and external customer relationships with clarity of purpose within collaborative, healthy cultures.

A founding co-partner of Market Impact, he is the host of the weekly podcast series Market Impact Insights, recognized by Forrester as a Top 100 Channel Podcast, sharing leadership best practices from around the world.

Dan lives in Snohomish, Washington with his wife Nikolett and two dogs. In his spare time, he enjoys workouts and hikes, reading, and is a passionate follower of college football.

BE AN IMPACT MAKER

In business, it's all about making a positive impact every day.

Be inspired by the voices of more than 75 leaders from around the world sharing key learnings from their journey to exceptional leadership, including:

- Building vibrant cultures of innovation
- Developing authentic, trusted relationships
- Embracing diversity
- Improving strategic decision-making by leveraging data
- Demonstrating leadership behaviors that generate exceptional results
- The power of optimism

Once you commit to engaging and serving others ... get ready to be amazed by all that is possible.

The
Impact
Makers

voices of leadership

DAN ALBAUM

The Impact Makers

Project Manager: Harry Brelsford
Design and Production: Yvonne Betancourt
Graphics: Anne Garrett

Paperback: 979-8-218-06572-0

Market Impact Press
20711 113th Drive SE
Snohomish, WA 98296
206-790-2760

List of Chapters

DEDICATION

For my family: Nikolett, Chelsey, Adam, Haley, Marianna and Julianne. You are my universe and a reminder that each moment of this life is precious.

ACKNOWLEDGMENTS

No project of this scope can be accomplished alone. I am grateful for the unwavering support of so many that have provided unconditional encouragement and inspiration.

First and foremost, my close friend and executive recruiter emeritus Tom Walker, who helped convince me a book was within my grasp; my editor and guide on this journey, Harry Brelsford, who has provided invaluable wisdom throughout the entire process of concept to page; my talented design and layout team who brought visual concepts to life, including Anne Garrett, Tara Brown, Yvonne Betancourt, and Julianne Bacso; the talented proofreading tandem of Gita Sharma and Hayley Galver; my sister Lisa, whose positive feedback and humor has kept me going through the most challenging times; my former business colleague Mike Stumvoll, who has provided such a positive business and spiritual sounding board; and my personal trainer, Kristina Teasley, who has been relentless in ensuring my wellness of both mind and body.

My immense gratitude extends to all of the guests, the Impact Makers, on my *Market Impact Insights* podcast I have been fortunate to interview, and have taught me so much about life, leadership, and making a positive impact every day. To all the exceptional team members that I have had the privilege to work with in companies large and small, thank you for the feedback, positive energy, and hard work enabling us to accomplish so much together.

And of course, I am most grateful for my wife and business partner Nikolett Bacso-Albaum, who amazes me every day with her grace, intelligence, and warmth, reminding me to dream big and that all things are possible.

FOREWORD

In the late 1990s, I relocated my family from the Midwest to Seattle to take my second job as a software engineer. The company, Active Voice, was well stocked with brilliant engineers that I had the privilege of learning from. More importantly, the executive team was incredibly focused on what is now called servant leadership – putting the needs of the team, customers, investors, and others before yourself.

Soon after I arrived, Dan was hired as the Director of Marketing for the product I was helping build. Initially, Dan struck me as even odder than the rest of the leaders. He was always asking: "How are you doing?," "How are your children doing?," and "Are you taking care of yourself?" He remembered the details of our prior conversations and was incredibly sincere. As an early career engineer, I did not look forward to meetings with sales and marketing – but I always had time for my new friend Dan.

Soon after, he began bringing customer stories that were rich and insightful. His genuine interest led people to open up and share insights I rarely got from others. The insights he gleaned were always human, and unique, yet always grounded in data and were crucial to many of the innovations we built into our products.

Later, Active Voice was acquired by Cisco Systems, the networking giant from Silicon Valley. Dan, I, and many others were suddenly small fish in a very large pond. Dan and I did not work together as often, but when we did, it was always the same: Dan seemed delighted to talk to me again, had made many rich connections within Cisco, and had customer insights that were rich, valuable, different, and allowed us to create solutions that resonated with our customers.

We often talked about the amazing innovations we helped create at Cisco, the leaders we worked with and their styles, the relationships we formed in our time there, and the unbridled optimism we felt, even during difficult times, that we were doing good for the world around us.

While Cisco was an amazing experience for both of us, eventually we both moved on to new challenges at other companies. Over time, I have had the privilege of serving as an executive in some exciting companies. I found myself consistently contacting Dan when I needed deeper insights into the interplay between people, technology, and strategy. He was always there for me and always had insights that were both unique and valuable.

When he started the Market Impact Insights podcast a few years ago, I was hooked. Dan was inviting us all into his special style of connecting, caring, and getting insights others miss. I rarely miss an episode and learn from his amazing guests but especially from the approach he uses.

A few months ago, Dan told me that he was writing a

book covering the interactions between Innovation, Relationships, Diversity, Data, Exceptional Leadership, and Optimism. And it would recap many of the salient points from his guests on the podcast as well as insights from his successful career. I was extremely excited and wanted to read the book immediately.

Based on my 30+ years of experiencing leaders and becoming one myself, Dan has identified the key ingredients for something special. Certainly these contribute to financial success but also for something deeper. At the intersection of Innovation, Relationships, Diversity Data, Leadership, and Optimism lies a bit of magic. It is the magic that allows for a more fulfilling life for oneself and the people around us.

Dan is one of the first caring, helpful, humble leaders I met. Today, we call the rare people like this servant leaders, and Dan is one of the best. I will always be thankful for his insights, and friendship, and for taking the time to show us a path to making our world a little better. I hope you find his book as inspiring as I did.

Joe Burton
CEO, Telesign

A COLD WINTER

"You will never make it in marketing."

The words cut through my soul as I gazed through the office glass at chilly November winds that were a staple of another Winter in the Northeast. It hurt even more that they came from the mouth of my manager, the other end of a recently formed relationship I had been furtively trying to strengthen.

Nine months earlier, I had been full of excitement after having been recruited to my Associate Product Manager role in a leading consumer packaged goods company by a charismatic, creative and collaborative Product Manager . But following some unexpected restructuring and musical chairs resulting in my receiving a new manager, here I was in a 1:1 conversation from hell about my future.

I was young and still relatively inexperienced in the professional world, having made a shift a few years before from the radio broadcasting business (code for long hours and low entry-level pay) to the MBA program at the University of Texas in Austin to junior marketing roles in the food and beverage market. Lacking confidence, small mistakes that should be part of a continuing and natural learning process was internalized and created a lot of personal anguish and stress. That my new manager was an isolated, unhappy soul with a negative demeanor who critiqued without praise and made fatalistic declarations was the ultimate high-octane fuel being poured on my fire daily.

As painful as the conversation was, it was a seminal moment in my mindset and future development as a leader. Having grown up in the laid-back Pacific Northwest, I was used to a highly supportive and empowering family, circle of friends, teachers and other employers that had "lifted my wings" through life's ups and downs. I wasn't used to having someone in a more senior role I should be looking up to be so intentionally destructive. Yes, I was imperfect on my job, struggling to find my voice in a competitive marketing environment in a place 3,000 miles from the comforts of my support system but this felt markedly different than "constructive" professional development.

But ultimately, I realized the deflation, the marginalization and being beat up over many months in this working relationship was more a reflection of *them*, not *me*. This was about propping up their fragile psyche by trying to break my spirit. I made a promise to myself in that moment of a dead-end future with that reporting relationship: When I had the opportunity to lead functions and people, I was going to be a very different kind of leader. I was going to be a servant leader who relentlessly inspired while removing barriers to ensure my team members grew and contributed in ways even they may not have felt was possible. I was going to proactively seek new learning opportunities in the pursuit of making a positive impact every day. I was going to *lift* instead of *deflate*.

And it just so happens that over the past 33 years I've stayed true to that promise. Through amazing prosperity with recognition and laughter in very successful B2B-focused organizations and consulting practice or through both sides of tearful conversations (can you say "layoffs"?), my determination to be an unbreakable leadership anchor for team success is stronger than ever. With world chaos all around us (global pandemic, military conflicts, political divides) providing new challenges for the next generation, there is no better time to follow through on my commitment as a servant leader to share the lessons of my multi-decade journey and offer the gift of the best quotes from the nearly one hundred accomplished leaders from all facets of business who I have been blessed to interview on *Market Impact Insights* podcast over the past three years.

This book is written for everyone looking to make a positive impact every day, whether you are young in your career or deep in your career looking for additional inspiration. In the coming pages, I will share many voices of experience around six foundational aspects of making a true impact: *Innovation, Relationships, Diversity, Data, Exceptional Leadership,* and *Optimism.*

I hope you find motivation whether you are strategizing and executing in a large enterprise, a small to medium size business, or an entrepreneur seeking sustainable growth for an infant business.

So strap in and fasten your seat belts. It's time to hear from the Impact Makers. Let's go!

THE INNOVATION ENGINE

---

in·no·va·tion – *a new method, product, idea, etc.*

Talk to leaders in any successful company and they will tell you that a culture that values innovation will ultimately generate the ideas that create meaningful market differentiation fueling long-term revenue and profit growth. Seems simple enough. Yet building and maintaining true innovation is one of the hardest things leaders face. In a 2019 McKinsey survey, 94 percent of executives are dissatisfied with their innovation performance.

What is the biggest challenge that makes sustainable innovation so elusive?

It's not one thing, but many hurdles…including a lack of clarity in vision, low employee motivation, siloed innovation efforts, a lack of cross-team collaboration, and inconsistent customer engagement. Add to that the constantly shifting dynamics of a volatile marketplace which only adds more headwind to your teams' innovation efforts. Or does it?

Don Proctor, founder, and CEO of Bk97 Digital, knows all about innovation in a competitive market having led a

1

multi-billion-dollar collaboration business at Cisco.

He also served as the CEO for the Center for Cisco Heritage—responsible for the historical legacy of this global technology giant—and is a noted lecturer at top universities. Proctor is a student of history. And history shows us some of the most amazing innovations—and massive missed opportunities—have come when mature markets go through periods of intense disruption.

So often the difference between winning and losing the race to market share in emerging technologies is defined not by what leaders can't see, but by how well they respond to what they can see.

Case in point: Kodak. As Proctor has shared in some of his on-campus guest lectures, this iconic 100-year-old brand missed seizing market leadership in an emerging market. Kodak developed some of the earliest digital cameras in the 1970s but missed the boat on fully committing to the commercialization of digital photography products.

"It wasn't just a matter of top leadership being asleep at the switch" he explains. "It was a far more subtle transformation in which they saw the industry structure changing, but were unable to adapt to the changes." In this painful case, internal inertia caused by the complacency of having an impressive legacy as a leading brand in a well-defined yet rapidly changing market—was a deterrent to act decisively and timely.

So how do companies—and more specifically, leaders—avoid inertia when sustainable market leadership calls for dynamic change?

Being intentional about creating a culture that fosters and rewards innovation is a great place to start. And that culture building isn't about senior leadership just saying the right things, it is about making sure time and resources are being applied to processes to bring greater accountability and actionability to innovative ideas being generated. Sometimes making a career decision to jump into a hyper-competitive market, and going to a place where courageous "outside the box" thinking is a non-negotiable requirement is the perfect motivator for developing an innovative and growth-oriented mindset.

I saw this first hand in the wireless industry at US West-AirTouch-Verizon Wireless during the hyper-growth of the late 1990s. Those of us working within the walls of ever-changing brands due to mergers and acquisitions affectionately called it the "Wild Wild West" and it was a time of continuous innovation, from mobile device form factors (think smaller) and enhanced services.

There was a strong cultural vibe of empowerment at AirTouch, with an intent to grow the business through a balanced foundation of financial, customer, operational, and people measures (a true "Balanced Scorecard"). This ultimately extended into being more transparent with customers in the form of an AirTouch "Brand Promise" campaign. It's amazing what people and teams can accomplish when they know they have the confidence of senior leadership—with clear accountability for generating innovative ideas and making key decisions to deliver sustainable growth.

Jim Liggett, who worked at McCaw Cellular, the predecessor of AT&T Wireless (and later a founder and

CEO of fitness innovator Stages Cycling) found that a growth mindset has been a key to his successful leadership journey. "What made a mark on me is the importance of growth in a new business" he explains. "There's a lot of things you need to do with your organization and the way you manage, but finding a business category that will grow and has a lot of momentum as a category is really an important ingredient. You don't have that many years to make a difference."

For me, the working frenzy in such crazy times when competitive movement happened in weekly or monthly increments versus annual increments, was calmed by the operational discipline of a simple yet powerful process for turning new product ideas into revenue-generating initiatives. The New Product Council process at USWest NewVector Group encouraged the breaking down of functional silos and ensuring senior leadership alignment in support of the company vision. The foundation was a documented "Stage Gate" approach to new product development, where senior leader approved decisions at each milestone in the life of the product idea to the product launch cycle (Concept, Product Definition/ Requirements, Go/No Go for launch, etc.) was done consistently, with "in the same room" voices of debate and discussion to ensure alignment and support for approved projects.

Whether it's a more formal multi-stage process, or more ad-hoc cross-functional product development reviews, an effective innovation culture benefits from having structure around a clear vision for decisions on where to apply development resources.

Barry Issberner, VP Marketing & Business Development at Almasons has been driving successful product development and hundreds of product launches for decades, including at Motorola, Intermec (now Honeywell), Avaya, and Datalogic. For him, living by a "Five Rules" code for translating innovative ideas into launchable products has come from the blood, sweat, tears, and triumph of learning in the trenches in organizations that have pushed out high volumes of products, sometimes as many as 60 a year!

According to Issberner, leaders with high-volume launch cycles "better have some good processes to try to coordinate those launches because you can't just treat each one as a unique snowflake. So, step (rule) one is tackling the fuzzy frontend…and doing it as quickly as possible." Achieving clarity from the fuzziness here is one of the hardest parts of the whole development process and is about gaining a deep understanding of your target markets, and the needs/pain points of your customers, along with the size and cost of problems. Feasibility analysis, making choices about development options that can address needs and can it be delivered at a price the customer can pay, and be at a price where the company can make a profit.

Issberner's second rule is all about following a very clear process for doing the product introduction, a clear and logical series of steps over several months:

- educating internal support teams (at least six months pre-launch)
- then your sales teams (at least three months pre-launch)

- talking to critical distys/system integrators (additional fuel in your sales channel)
- talking to resellers/ISVs (who buy through distys/integrators)
- engaging with key influencers: the press and analysts (the initial source of awareness for many prospects)
- then public launch (with a goal of everyone being fired up simultaneously!)

Successful tech launches follow this order consistently and avoid the temptation to reveal new products prematurely at a major trade show/event. As Barry says, "Do not uncork the wine prematurely!"

The third rule is being clear internally on concrete goals post-launch for the first 12 months, including revenue goals, market penetration targets and more. This can be a challenging step and should happen as early in the overall launch planning process as possible. Sometimes the defined goals can be underwhelming to senior leadership and can deflate C-suite support. A one-page summary approach, with "green/yellow/red" status indicators, creates a dynamic launch checklist— including documenting (and tracking ongoing progress with) major accounts that are the most likely prospects and creates greater accountability around the overall goals for the product.

Figure 1.1 Go-To-Market Status Chart

GO-TO-MARKET STRATEGY TEMPLATE for SaaS

ACTIVITY	STATUS	ASSIGNED TO	START DATE	END DATE	NOTES
PHASE 1: PLANNING					
Establish Goals	Complete				
Determine Target Audience	In Progress				
Develop Creative Concept	Overdue				
Identify Marketing Channels	Not Started				
Budget and Financial Projection	On Hold				
Set Up Campaign Calendar	Needs Review				
Develop Plan for Testing					
Creative Brief					
PHASE 2: CREATIVE DEVELOPMENT					
Message Planning					
Create Marketing Assets					
Gather Customer Testimonials					
Other					
PHASE 3: PROMOTION PLAN					
Email Campaign					
Social Media					
Sales Outreach					
Other					
PHASE 4: TESTING					
Split Testing					
Results Analysis					
Plan Refinement					
Other					
PHASE 5: LAUNCH					
Channel A					
Channel B					
Channel C					
Channel D					
PHASE 6: MEASUREMENT					
Key Metrics Channel A					
Key Metrics Channel B					
Performance Evaluation					
Plan Refinement					

The fourth rule is diligent communication to key stakeholders, including your client-facing teams and other functional groups and partners including Legal. Getting your internal reviews and debate done BEFORE a product is publicly visible is key. Be very transparent about any ads, moves or changes on the rolling launch planning calendars every few weeks. Document, document, document.

And the fifth rule is extending your close watch on new products for at least the first year after the initial launch. Document where things go off course, and take the learning to heart in the spirit of actions that drive continuous improvement.

While having a well-defined, repeatable process is essential for getting the most from your company's innovation efforts, recruiting the right people to play key roles within the process is also an essential ingredient in producing results.

Kathryn Robinson, Chief Growth Officer at Fexa, knows this all too well from her extensive digital media innovation experience at Turner Broadcasting and the business development of adjacent-to-core markets at Cisco. It still comes down to the human factor. And for her, the greatest impact when innovating with complex new technologies has come when teams avoid becoming infatuated with the "cool factor" or buzzwords (can you say "AI" or "machine learning"?) and stay focused on the actual customer problem they are trying to solve.

"Outcomes and results happen when you have the deep technical expertise but you also have the synthesizers and connectors coming into the equation," Robinson says. "These are people who have the capability to bring pockets of expertise across teams together with a market-sensing customer empathy and understanding."

These synthesizers and connectors in your organization can carry a wide range of titles, from a customer success rep who has a finger on the pulse of customer needs to a market researcher who has gained relevant, valuable insights from focus groups, 1:1 conversations, or online surveys.

Innovation also extends to your own and your team members' continuous learning.

Accomplished entrepreneur and business strategist **Sharon Richardson-Howell Ph.D.**, who worked with me on some of our biggest wireless innovations at AirTouch including pre-paid cellular, is a strong believer in deep self-introspection and a term first coined by her professor Dr. David J. Teece of UC-Berkeley as "negative knowledge". Your growth as a team is about so much more than just celebrating success.

"It's about the knowledge of failure", she says. "You know how you progress through knowing how something has failed. And I think it takes you much farther than the knowledge of success. It certainly creates more learning opportunities but you have to be able to put your arms around that past of yours. While change is seen as hard and difficult, transformation is something different. Transformation can be kind of like a butterfly."

Being transformational with your innovation initiatives means making decisions about where to say "yes" to financial investment in projects and when to say "no". Which is hard for most people.

John Traynor is a product marketing veteran, leading technology teams at Microsoft and currently as VP & GM of a product at TensorIoT. He agrees with the legendary management consultant Peter Drucker that abandonment decisions with many potentially innovative projects in the development pipeline are one of the toughest decisions a product leader can make.

"In order to ensure your success you do need to decide what NOT to do," Traynor says. "I had an executive who used to talk about the tyranny of 'or'…being told we had to do this or that…and his retort was I want to do this and that. I want to do them all. It's fine to have great aspirations, but at least let's agree on an order to do them in. The times I've been most successful is when there have been a relatively small set of goals and objectives."

The same issue plagues startups that are pitching for venture capital and in their pursuit of the best optics, they may commit to too much. Of course, sometimes the push for meaningful innovation by entrepreneurs is inspired by an unexpected life event.

Billy Price, Founder of BILLY Footwear, suffered a life-changing spinal injury in an accidental three-story fall from a building that rendered him a quadriplegic at age 18. And the frustration and limitations of not having a viable way to ease his feet unobstructed into his shoes over the next 18 years helped birth a unique shoelace-free design now available through several major retailers including Nordstrom and Zappos that is changing the lives of people around the world. His drive for innovation born from a personal need translates into a culture that values the customer's voice. Having a relatively small team meant committing to technology for manufacturing and supply chain flexibility and the innovation engine in the intensely competitive shoe market requires constant discipline in decision-making as growth is through by category expansion.

"Every time we made leaps, it was a real financial crunch because you have to stretch yourself basically as far as you can go, but not necessarily as far as the customer wants you to go," Price shares. "That's where the balance between doing everything you want to do but just having to be fiscally responsible to be able to survive as a business and make the next push."

Price's company participated in startup incubator The Batchery, whose CEO **Peter Burghardt** has evaluated hundreds of emerging company business plans and approaches to innovation. Peter agrees that establishing a strong cultural foundation is critical to fostering healthy innovation.

"Culture starts early on," he says. "It might just be you, your cofounder, and a dog. The trick is to set it and to enshrine it early on to make sure it jives with the direction of the company, the ethos of the company, that it creates an atmosphere conducive to collaboration allowing for ideas to percolate up and making people feel valued."

Great innovation isn't only about ideas generated by your internal staff. The voice of your customers can be a powerful catalyst. Of course, making sure your teams are in a position to collect and really listen to that customer input is the real difference. And often, the tone is set from the highest levels in the organization, beginning with the CEO.

Pat Byrne is VP of Lean Transformation and Safety for GE. Formerly the CEO of GE Digital and GE Renewables Onshore Wind, he is a strong proponent of continuously engaging with customers to better understand their business, and their needs and enable them to provide input into their customer experience and your roadmap.

While a member of his team at Intermec (now Honeywell), I was always amazed at the amount of time Byrne carved out for customer visits, group meetings, or 1:1 dinners. He has made customer interactions a cornerstone in his career development. He appreciated early on how deep customer engagement and understanding are the lifeblood of continuous improvement and innovation, and his later experiences at GE Digital serve as a great example.

"We pivoted our organization...towards being more of an industry-focused customer workflow-oriented business. We really wanted to be deep in our customers," Byrne reflects. "The best way to really understand our customers' priorities is to live with our customers to understand what really drives their metrics and what works in their organization. What are some of the challenges that they have and what are the places where they're looking to get a breakthrough in results? It's not only a technology immersion, it's really understanding our customers' business priorities, their business processes, their initiatives and engaging with on those to understand where are the opportunities to make a difference."

It takes time and extra effort for sure, but the benefits of reaching that deeper customer understanding are compelling, including accelerated and more agile development plus the ability to continuously iterate in conducting rapid experimentation.

Byrne concedes this customer immersion process doesn't necessarily produce a flawless product and delivers "maybe not a perfect solution, but a concept on what our teams can do to drive a particular outcome. This allows a level of flexibility, resilience, and mobility in the innovation and agility becomes a key part of the immersion and source of competitive advantage. The teams get to know each other, invest in each other, and innovate together."

When the C-Suite of an organization sets the tone in valuing customer time, it sends a strong message across the company on the priority of getting quality customer feedback and ideas that impact everything from operations to product roadmaps. It intellectually challenges the entire organization, it goes beyond the reliance on that one person who is "the smartest person in the room" and it projects a long-term view on things—24, 36, 48 months or longer.

The greatest impact comes when outside-the-box thinking can come proactively, versus reactively.

Alan Cohen is a Partner at DCVC, helping create billions of dollars of value through his investment and his firm's portfolio of technology companies. With a long track record of executive management at Airespace, Cisco, Illumio, and Nicira, Alan is a vocal champion for the value of anticipating, versus just reacting—especially in intensely competitive, highly dynamic technology markets.

"You never envision something happens until something really severe happens and then that forces you to change your pattern, that's the reactive mode," he observes. "The question is anticipating the changes which is the really hard work for all of us so you can adapt and vector toward those directions that are going to be more resilient."

Of course, it's one thing to proactively anticipate market changes, foster internal innovation and develop a new solution. But especially for young companies, the ability to attract investors can circle back to being able to demonstrate a deeper understanding of customer needs and the barriers to adoption than bigger, incumbent competitors.

Cohen is very specific in his approach to evaluating new investment opportunities.

"I look at teams that really dig in to both the technology and market size, teams that have diversity in skills and human beings. Because you're either trying to figure out something that never existed before or how to take on a significant incumbent in a sector where they may be very dominant," he says.

How your company externally communicates what it innovates and how you target the market in growing awareness and adoption also matters.

"Then I look for strong go-to-market plans, you know there is the old adage saying how do you eat an elephant? They say one very small bit at a time so you don't really attack the market broadly you attack them very narrowly in the beginning. History is replete with great technologies who couldn't figure out how to take something to go to market and less compelling technology may win by a team that have actually figured those parts out."

So the question remains, are organizations more

naturally prone to innovation due to having an employee population that carries the natural traits of collaboration, creativity, and positive energy? Or just maybe there are intentional steps that can be taken to build a culture with values that creates more engaged employees that can better contribute to ongoing innovation.

Employees that care are employees that are more likely to deliver innovative ideas. And with various surveys showing as few as only about one-third of employees being fully engaged on average, there is a huge gap in achieving full innovation potential.

Chris Litherland, an HR leader at several global technology companies and founder of Mariposa Consulting, has realized the power of highly engaged teams over 20 years of being asked to measure and help business leaders boost performance. This is not just about measuring happiness and morale; it needs to be linked to business performance and the business environment.

"Our desire and ability to contribute, collaborate and perform at our best. In a team context, it's determined by our perception of our work, the tasks we've been asked to complete, towards our leadership," Litherland reflects.

"How we see the value of our organization…or not…in terms of its value and culture. You get the wrong culture, the wrong misalignment on values, you'll see employees disengage very quickly."

This isn't just about an HR-led initiative. Recruiting, developing and retaining highly engaged employees is all about connection and collaboration across the business, bridging the business, and leveraging the existing internal knowledge. Creating energy, and driving innovation comes through cross-functional initiatives. As Gallup polls have noted, more highly engaged employees are less likely to turnover, which also contributes to greater innovation and overall productivity.

Disengaged employees can undermine innovation in another way…internal security threats either through lax practices that expose the company to risks or through malicious intent.

Litherland calls out some key best practices for avoiding obstacles and increasing engagement:

- long term holistic approach: not falling into the trap of developing one-time only employee programs, and being intentional in coordinating efforts across your organization
- focused investments, with qualitative and quantitative measurement: getting executive team buy-in, with specific goal setting
- culture value chain: people-centered building blocks for how you do business, then the impact on employees and ultimately customers. Make your business easier for employees and your customers.

Even as you engage your employees, you must be continuously recruiting and developing the right blend of capabilities across your organization. A blending of science with art. This is especially true if you are in the intensely competitive B2B technology space. A question that leaders need to answer is whether their teams have reached a fully matured state in terms of their skillsets and their understanding of the marketing stack.

William Toll, a 25-year veteran of the tech space who heads up Product Marketing at ReversingLabs, calls the elusive, game-changing inflection point when analytic, technical, and creative skills within a team are fully realized the "Maturity Gate". This provides a special kind of optimism through the inevitable roller coaster ride of technology startups where the best-laid plans encounter unexpected headwinds, twists, and turns.

Figure 1.2 Rollercoaster chart

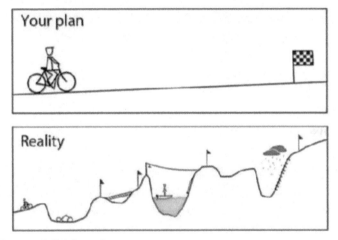

Source: PJM Consulting

"You have these really dark days where it just seems nothing can be done and you're not making any progress and can't get your story through and there's product issues and customer issues," he says. "Then there are these 'oh my god' days, look what we just did with great coverage in the media, with the analysts and all the right things' because you just get to these gates."

Emerging technologies like Artificial Intelligence (AI) will be another forcing function for organizations to develop ever-expanding skillsets to remain competitive, and even relevant.

Christi DeCuir is an engineering and business development leader who has spent the past 20 years working with cutting-edge technologies, including more than a decade with Cisco and most recently with NVIDIA. With amazing advances in AI that are transforming everything in our daily lives from natural language translation, employed by your loyal friends Alexa and Siri, to computer vision that tracks consumer location in retail, winning companies need employees that have skills supporting a more strategic set of objectives.

"You really need to build a skillset of being a visionary and that means being creative and being a creative abstract problem solver," she advises. "I think there's not many people like that today."

Beyond having a creative mindset with an eye toward the future, DeCuir also believes in the power of having builders on your team with the constructive and executional abilities to make your company's vision a reality. One way to accelerate building solutions from great ideas is to leverage sizeable external technical communities that have a passion for a baseline technology your company utilizes. In NVIDIA's case, this means partnering with AWS on a series of "Hackathons", contests where anyone with the requisite technical skills can take part by thinking of a relevant problem and coming up with their own solution.

Not only are the ideas generated at these contests often golden, but they can also be catalysts for developing breakthrough new relationships that benefit both the builders and the hosts.

"You would not believe the innovation that unfolds, it really is astounding to see what people can do as a team or as individuals in a short period of time," DeCuir observes. "Some of those ideas that have come out of these events have led to collaborative engagements."

By harnessing greater innovation from your employees and external partnerships, several positive things happen—including being able to transform your user experiences into a competitive advantage. That doesn't mean this transformation comes easily, without collaboration or risks.

But it's worth it, according to **Phillip Hunter** who has spent decades in passionate pursuit of perfecting innovative user experiences, including at Amazon, Microsoft, and most recently as Director of User Experience at Collibra. Philip argues that the user experiences you deliver are an important representation of who you are as a brand and in essence an extension of your brand promise. And a key factor in effectively incorporating the voice of the customer into your innovation is working across functional lines.

In the case of Amazon and the very popular Alexa user experience, Hunter's understanding of two distinct customers – end users experiencing it in their homes and developers building new functionality for the experience – was vital. It all started with asking his marketing teams the right set of questions.

"How are you going to talk to these people? How are we trying to engage them? How are we going to support them the best?" I was able to take the answers to these questions and turn them into features and product needs," he says. "And then there were other times where I was able to say 'hey I've been in the speech recognition world for a long time and I've worked with many developers and many kinds of development teams. So here are some of the things that I think that I know that they need in this new world.'

By proactively sharing his perspective on the "careabouts" of these distinct audiences, Hunter was able to enlighten his marketing team to create stronger end-user connection and help motivate developers to build better things, faster.

Speaking of fast, another area accelerating during the pandemic is mergers and acquisitions (M&A). According to Reactiv, global M&A activity returned with a vengeance in 2021 from a COVID-impacted 2020, climbing 82% globally to a record $5.9 trillion in value through 63,000 transactions.

All this activity, generating so much financial value across intensely competitive markets, begs an important question: what can innovative companies do to maximize perceived value with investors and potential acquirers?

According to **Jonathan Shroyer**, a proven entrepreneur who as CEO recently led the sale of the company he co-founded, Officium Labs, to Arise Virtual Solutions in the gaming space, look no further than aspirational, savvy marketing tactics to elevate your profile.

"Our thought process was that if people don't know us, let's figure out how to leverage marketing to fight a couple of levels above our belt," he says. "If we're kind of a minnow in the pond and we are a welterweight, how do project we have heavyweight status? We really leveraged marketing from day one to do that, through social proof marketing, through thought leadership conferences, through blogs, through podcasts, and really projecting that while we may be small people are going to think we're bigger because we have that capability inside to be bigger."

Another key ingredient of Shroyer's successful path to acquisition was a startup hiring strategy that put a premium on candidates having at least 15-20 years of industry experience, which meant recruited talent brought in more established professional networks from day one with the ability to drive deeper impact.

"We needed our new talent to be t-shaped employees, which means they can go deep in one area and then wide across with large established networks we could sell and grow the business faster," Shroyer says.

Figure 1.3 Acquisition Coupons

"No, it's fine, I've just never seen coupons used in an acquisition."

Source: Mark Anderson

Beyond a commitment to perception-changing marketing and talent acquisition strategies, there is another internal element that highly innovative companies have and that is a "stage-ready" mindset that appreciates, and leverages the power of marketing.

Shroyer recalls a former boss who mentored him on the importance of staying alert and mentally sharp. "He used to say, you're always on stage and you never know when the curtains open so you should always pretend it is open." The same is true of companies. In a sense, they are on one long, continuous stage and every bit of public content that is communicated, regardless of whether it is through paid or organic channels, will be marketing influenced. This influence extends to include recruitment of employees, investors and potential acquirers.

"Marketing plays a critical role," Shroyer observes. "I don't know how companies can be super successful in this day and age if they don't understand the power of marketing."

Sometimes successful innovation means finding a different yet meaningful niche in a mature market.

Troy Trenchard has seen it all as a senior leader in several successful technology companies, including Cisco, and Avaya and formely as CMO at Sonatus, delivering advanced intelligence to automobiles including a strategic partnership with Hyundai.

In a hotly competitive global market with massive innovation happening before our eyes where cars are increasingly powered through electricity versus petroleum, Sonatus is truly changing the game via its' software to enable a "smarter" driving experience.

For Trenchard, innovation and a collaborative mindset are intertwined, where the outside influence of a partner can be a huge catalyst for transformation. Case in point: Hyundai.

"If you look at where they were forty years ago right to where they are now, they build some of the most highly rated cars in the world. Especially the Genesis line. They had to learn how to be nimble and build a lot of skillsets and expertise. That's not just in the culture but in the process and how you do things" he says.

"Being a startup and being software-focused and highly agile we work very differently. One of the key parts to being successful in the role that we play is not just a supplier but actually kind of a change agent in learning how to work with them." Trenchard reflects.

"In the early meetings, we undoubtedly looked like aliens because we talked about agile processes and sprints and being able to implement evolving requirements in two weeks or four weeks or six weeks. It's been a great opportunity to work with people who are experts in their field and bring them new ways of thinking about and doing things and a couple of years into working with them, we can see how they've evolved as well."

Whether you're cultivating amazing innovations inside your company or evolving to more progressive thinking through the influence of your strategic partners, those innovations are some of your most precious assets. It's the unique blend or "secret sauce" that enables competitive advantage. And exceptional leaders make sure to put the proper focus on absolutely, positively protecting those intellectual assets.

Phyllis Turner-Brim has spent decades as a technical product leader and corporate counsel at Procter & Gamble, General Electric, and Starbucks, and is currently Deputy General Counsel and Chief Intellectual Property (IP) Officer at multi-billion-dollar global technology giant HP Inc.

She lives in a very active patent world; according to the World Intellectual Property Organization (WIPO) there were about 278,000 patent applications globally in 2021, setting a new record. According to research by Insights by Grey 8, HP filed more than 2,000 patent applications in a single year as recently as 2015 alone. Thus, a total of more than 22,000 patents (active plus inactive) worldwide.

Assuming they take the key first step in recognizing intellectual asset protection as a company priority in supporting continuous innovation, there are still some very common pitfalls companies fall into. One of the biggest is managing their IP process as a separate silo.

"The most important thing is to understand that the IP strategy is connected to business strategy. Before I can help my clients develop an IP strategy, I first have to what are your business goals" she says. Turner-Brim is mystified that IP work is often handled completely separate from what is going on in the business, especially given its' high relative cost.

"The business of my business is not the legal department. Not the IP department. The business of the business is defined by business leaders. How can we bring IP in to support that? It should be right at the table as we are defining the business strategy. Frequently, IP is just thought of as an afterthought."

By bringing IP experts into their strategic business planning early and often, companies can reduce expenses and boost the productivity of counsel in pursuit of asset protection.

TAKEAWAYS CHECKLIST:

☑ Take an action-biased mindset that still includes the discipline to say "no"

☑ Commit to a consistent, repeatable process for product development

☑ Break down silos by leveraging marketing and your IP staff in the earliest stages of your business strategic planning

2

RELATIONSHIPS ARE EVERYTHING

---

re·la·tion·ship – *the way in which two or more concepts, objects, or people are connected, or the state of being connected.*

Once you've created or contributed to an environment that is ripe with meaningful innovation, reaching your team's and company's full potential is all about creating and nurturing healthy trusted relationships. Meaningful relationships with your internal stakeholders, prospects, customers, channel, ecosystem, and technology partners are everything.

Building strong relationships doesn't come easy, whether at a personal, team, or organizational level. Creating strong connections takes relentless commitment and continuous self-awareness. It's about recognizing we're all part of an interconnected "human ecosystem" that begins with self, and family and extends to our social networks, schools, business colleagues, corporate boards, business partners, prospective or existing customers, and our communities at large.

Do you want to make a positive impact every day? Understand and start investing in your human ecosystem by building authentic, trusted relationships that are enduring and provide mutual growth.

Of course, ensuring the overall emotional and physical well-being of parties in any relationship is a huge factor for success. Related to personal wellness, there has been a growing societal sensitivity and realization over the past decade about the importance of achieving "balance" between our personal and work lives. This has only been accentuated by the disruption and stress brought on by the global pandemic. Indeed, workaholic lifestyles that put bosses and jobs unconditionally above everything else in life are rightly recognized as unhealthy, leading to physical and emotional breakdown over time.

But in the realm of balance, it's also true that over-predictability and sameness in life routine can also lead to boredom and stagnation of mind and spirit.

Dan Thurmon, a nationally recognized leadership coach and speaker, suggests going "off balance" can be truly transformational in a positive way.

Thurmon should know, as his life story is the epitome of unconventional. As a former acrobatic performer, he incorporates amazing feats of concentration and circus-style acrobatics into his speaking performances to business audiences around the world. By doing this, he's demonstrating vividly the energy and vitality that comes with pushing yourself outside of your comfort zone. After spending a lot of time working in and around the C-suite of Fortune 500 companies he had a revelation.

"They said we really work hard toward trying to achieve work-life balance and it occurred to me that really is the wrong objective because balance is not something you ever achieve, balance is what you do," Thurmon says. "You're engaged throughout your life in that. In the process of making adjustments and changes and advocating for what's important at the moment and it's in those moments that we realize it's not about trying to achieve this state of complacency or perfection. We want to be off balance. We want to be engaged in what matters, we want to be present in the moments we experience and initiating the right changes to create the future we envision."

The message from Thurmon is simple. Be *intentional*. Be off balance on *purpose* to be proactive, not *reactive*, about what's happening around you in going after your best life and leadership impact.

Being intentional extends beyond self to connecting and building healthy relationships with others. *Networking* in its most simple form is defined as establishing a mutually beneficial relationship with other business people and potential clients or customers. Pretty straightforward right? Yet it is often neglected as a powerful tool in leadership development.

It's not about just the titles you earn. According to **Megan Roudebush**, founder of startup networking app keepwith, it's even more about the *company you keep*. Her original motivation for being a networking entrepreneur was observing the phenomenon of "device isolation" where people have become ever more fixated on interactions with their devices and losing touch with the art of authentic interpersonal connection. This became even more apparent as the pandemic, beginning in 2020, began pushing people in large organizations into greater physical isolation.

"We have helped people think more broadly about how they network using technology," she says. "The irony is it is now technology that is helping keep us together. As a founder, you always want to solve an actual problem in the world. Networking is hard, and that is the problem we are solving, and (with the pandemic) it got way harder."

Roudebush reminds us that networking is often about small, repetitive gestures, as simple as sending a daily text of gratitude to close friends or sending coffee to a friend or colleague working from home. But for many reasons, effective networking can be very challenging.

"We live in a time where the number of people you know, how many followers, how many likes, how many links you have defines us," she says. "It's that numbers approach that can sometimes be a roadblock to real, authentic relationship building. If we're truly talking about building and maintaining meaningful and reciprocal relationships, going deeper and paying more attention to fewer relationships and really cultivating them is a better move."

This means being more discerning about who you allow into your networks. She emphasizes that the people with whom you surround yourself, the "company that you keep," become a reflection of your brand. She's applied this for herself at keepwith, creating a self-described "Ocean's Eleven" team of skilled advisors. The key is to take a more disciplined, methodical, and strategic approach, where reciprocity reigns supreme over just a transactional mindset, and avoid the common pitfall of the "busy trap," where all the other competing noise in your life results in not making enough time to network.

Most of all, seizing opportunity. While many feel the onset of the global pandemic became restricting and isolating, Roudebush sees this as a great opportunity, allowing you to broaden your geographic reach and reach others in a way more authentic "work from home" environment versus a traditional office. She advises everyone to schedule a recurring weekly meeting invite for personal networking time, regardless of where you are. Turning strategic networking into a deep habit that supports your overall well-being.

"From a relationship-building perspective, we know having a strong network that has your back supports your overall wellness," Roudebush says. "There is a huge connection between networking and wellness. People will start to view networking as a healthy habit, and by spending time every week on their most meaningful relationships, they will recognize the positive wellness benefits."

So it's one thing to successfully develop your network with people *outside* your organization, but what about the key relationships *inside* your company? Human capital is the most precious asset in any successful organization, so fostering a culture where employees feel supported, valued, and given a chance to grow is critical for retention.

This is especially true in a highly disruptive, once-in-a-century pandemic environment where employees en masse are re-evaluating their priorities and exiting companies in record numbers. Dubbed the "Great Resignation" in the media, federal labor data shows nearly 48 million workers left their jobs in 2021, an all-time high. In a global Willis Towers Watson survey, nearly half (44%) of respondents admitted being in "job seeking" mode. These aren't performance-driven defections, this is all about setting uncompromising high standards for what workers want out of life and work.

So what can leaders do proactively to create the most productive and "sticky" relationships with their team members who are increasingly working in remote environments?

Keri Smith, Chief People Officer at engineering firm DOWL and an accomplished HR leader at several leading tech companies, says it starts with leaders having the right attitude.

"The biggest thing I've seen is their ability, desire, and understanding that they need to be flexible and adaptable as a leader and that they need to have empathy with their team members," she observes. "It's challenging right now to ensure your entire team is engaged and focused."

Something that has made a huge difference at DOWL is the intentional decision by senior leaders to have more frequent and meaningful interactions with their teams. Building off the company values of Innovation, Inspiration, Innovation, and Trust, a formal "check-in" process, separate from the traditional performance review tracking, creates interactive dialogue twice a year around two simple questions: "How are you doing?" and a second question to measure employee engagement.

Creating a culture that values conversational moments that are "real" and promote greater trust and a sense of well-being is important for the next generation of professional workers, Gen Z.

"One thing I tell people to keep in mind with Gen Z is they were born into a world where the United States had never been attacked by terrorists on its own soil. Beyond terrorist attacks, this generation has the most school violence that has ever occurred," Smith says. "For Gen Z the world is not as safe as what we all used to know when we grew up so psychological safety and well-being are really important."

Smith also notes a plus for this next generation is they are more naturally adaptable and flexible, strong digital natives so some of this technology is not a problem.

One employee group that has one of the most significant impacts on top-line revenue is your direct sales team. In highly competitive markets with nothing short of an "arms race" for top talent, what will make the difference for great leadership in helping those teams create more meaningful customer connections?

Laura Blackmer, President of Konica Minolta Dealer Sales, who has led the building of large-scale, high-impact strategic channel relationships for several global technology companies including HP, sees a distinct skill as critical to model for her sales teams: being "present."

"It can be taught, but there still needs to be a piece of the person who finds that to be a natural ability because you can't fake it. You can't pretend to be listening," she says. "They used to tell you to acknowledge what the other person is saying or nod your head or make eye contact. All of those things are great things to do, but they're not a replacement for really hearing what's happening in the environment immediately in front of you."

Ultimately, what happens *after* you are present in those key moments will be the most important in your sales relationships.

"Hopefully if I do it right and 'get it' then that information becomes priceless to me and I can take that information and do a million things with it that will add value because the reality is whether you're listening or not in the moment, most people may not be able to tell but what they will tell is did you actually do something meaningful with the information we just shared," Blackmer adds.

"There's no other way to measure it. It's not how many times I nod my head or I say aha. It's how much I can take that information and make something that really does hit the mark. Customers know the difference. It's probably the hardest thing we do as people especially now with all the distractions in front of us."

Figure 2.1 Listening

Consistently paying attention, listening empathetically, and being present in the moments with customers are typically reflective of "customer-focused" cultures. Leaders have a responsibility, but a tremendous opportunity, to model behaviors, and shape and reinforce the culture built around creating customer delight. Blackmer has found this especially challenging in a dynamic channel environment.

"Some of it's just figuring out who is our customer and I can tell you early on in my days in channels I spent a lot of time educating our company that the customer wasn't just the person that ultimately plugged this product into their wall and started using it," she says.

"The customer was everyone in that supply chain who was ultimately doing an action on our behalf and that took a while, there was a lot of resistance to thinking of distributors or resellers or dealers as customers. We wanted to think of them as a cog in the weel, a step in the chain, and the reality is there's a give and take at each level," she says.

Part of this equation is getting comfortable with the idea that you may not get it right 100% of the time, with the perseverance to keep trying and keep learning. Blackmer refers to this as the way to achieve what Randy Bean described in his book "fail fast, learn faster".

Sometimes developing the healthiest relationships with your employees is accelerated when the entire company has a common rallying point, an authentic description of cultural values that is easy to recite, easy to remember, and has a long shelf life.

For **Scott Smith**, co-Founder of software analytics innovator Qualtrics in his basement in 2002 and sold to technology giant SAP sixteen years later for $8 billion, the approach has been all about keeping things simple. In this case, being inspired by his son's experience at Google and the power of cultivating a very distinct culture, developing the concept of TACOS.

T represents being "transparent". A is "all in" (employee commitment). C means being "customer-obsessed and customer-centered". O is short for "one team". And "S" stands for "scrappy".

TACOS is not an internal marketing campaign, it is a guiding principle for how Qualtrics approaches its' work, its employees, and its customers.

The foundation of transparency at Qualtrics is readily apparent and pervasive.

"You can see there are no offices. Everyone has a desk. The CEO has a desk that's the same as everyone else and it's all out in the open," he says. "I can see everyone's screen and they can see mine and so forth. There are rooms where you can hold meetings but they are totally glass. You can see in there from any direction which protects every employee that is there," Smith says.

"If you're engaging in radical transparency, it really demands everyone is informed about what should be done and what is being done."

Smith is proud of what TACOS has created, from a customer obsession that never confuses doing what is right for the customer to a ubiquitous, unselfish commitment to teams that work extensively together on the hiring, evaluation, and mentoring of their members. Plus a scrappy mindset that is very focused on a particular outcome.

"We don't fail. We hate to lose, just a passion to win. And whatever we're doing, we've got smart people and we use this passion and the scrappiness to do things and do them in the right way."

Figure 2.2 TACOS

Building stronger employee relationships and loyalty is hard enough when overall business conditions are positive. What about when smooth seas become troubled waters when a company must deal with unexpected, dynamic shifts in the marketplace or crises that can potentially make leaders themselves more fragile?

Crisis communications and business leadership consultant **Stephynie Malik**, founder of SMALIK Enterprises, has worked as a business leadership consultant with major corporations generating billions of dollars a year annually, and her theory chaotic times, such as the pandemic, has driven leadership behaviors at the core of human relationships.

"It's not only how to pivot, it's how to lead transparently while building trust when you yourself are feeling as a leader anxious or unsure or insecure. How do you present in an amazing leadership way when you are feeling down?"

To evaluate the change needed, Malik applies a three-step process working with leaders dealing with tumultuous change. She admits it can be a bit tricky as it doesn't take away any of the emotion so there can still be a type of morning-over changes required in their business.

The first step is to *Assess* – where is the business, where is the journey?

The next step is about *Comfort* – what are the sacrifices and implications of the current situation? Is this about pivoting or a comprehensive change?

The final step is to *Assign and align* – Meet with key stakeholders quickly to define programs with outcomes associated with weekly goals established for ongoing accountability.

The real value of the process is its' creation of a tangible roadmap for action.

"You really have a plan set forth for your executives and for your team to actually begin to move forward through the trenches," she says.

Of course, managing relationships as part of building a healthy, strong company culture in times of great change or crisis is really hard. It often is not due to a lack of effort. Many companies spend significant money on getting consulting advice for culture development or program development but either choose not to *listen* to the recommendations, or perhaps are asking the wrong questions when surveying employees, or even if asking the right questions are getting less-than-honest employee answers.

At the end of the day, Malik advises focusing on three primary things to shift the culture in the direction you are seeking:

Know that your talent is your highest valued asset.

Have the integrity to *listen* even when you are wrong.

Have the ability to *act*, even if it is not your idea.

Beyond a focus on self, the authentic relationships

you build as you expand your network, and the strong relationships formed with your employees—including direct sales teams—another dimension that has a tremendous impact on your business is the healthy, product relationships you build with strategic partner organizations.

These partners often form a constellation within vast interconnected ecosystems, with mutual ambitions and desired outcomes. The key is to seamlessly partner in a way that enhances mutual customer experience and provides strategic growth for all parties.

Nancy Ridge is the Founder and President of Ridge Innovative, a consultancy helping companies leverage technology and innovation to achieve business outcomes. With nearly 30 years of experience understanding and optimizing IT channels, she sees a huge shift—accelerated the past few years with a global pandemic and the accelerated shift to virtual work environments—in how channel partners need to connect and thrive together. She notes may have chosen some time to "wait it out" but believes that downtime from a traditional in-office work environment should always be viewed as an opportunity to be productive.

So, what are the keys to keeping healthy productive channels, even during times of great disruption? It may be more straightforward than you think.

"It means going back to the basics," she says. "It begins with a vision. We need to enroll others. We have to connect. We have to communicate, which means listening often times more than talking. We have to create new

KPIs, new structures to manage and measure to solve problems."

There are the things we all *do* as part of working partnerships in channels, and there is a corresponding *mindset* we bring into everything we do that Ridge feels is easy to overlook. It all begins with maintaining a sense of relevance and understanding the needs of others.

"It's also important to be generous, and empathetic," Ridge notes. "Technology more than ever is now going to play a role in enabling not only business itself but certainly the channel and this really tells me that healthy channels are still going to be able to meet a need, that's going to be their primary purpose."

There are strong parallels in nature to the interconnected ecosystems in the business world, compelling examples that intentional relationships aren't nice to have for flourishing, they are vital for survival.

Ridge cites inspiration from "The Death of Competition" by James Moore in referring to examples of tidepools on the beach near her home as a vivid example. All of the microscopic organisms in and around these pools rely heavily on the tides and each other to survive, they find their purpose in each other and survive together. Similarly, the future of work in business ecosystems is based on the idea of collaboration and purpose with each other to collectively survive. Just like in nature, where changing weather conditions require adaptability at the moment and evolution over time, so too the best business partnership is ever-changing, growing, and evolving.

Figure 2.3 Tide Pools

Source: Fylling's Illustrated Guide to Pacific Coast Tide Pools

Just like in nature, our own families provide a powerful case study of the impact of supportive relationships. In the inevitable ups and downs of life, so many of us experience the highs and the lows, the good times and the not-so-good times. Within healthy families, each member draws strength from others to lift them up and collectively the unit becomes more resilient in navigating through life's storms (sometimes hurricanes!). This doesn't mean every member is a clone and there aren't divergent points of view and spirited debates. It means there is an inner confidence that builds over time that ultimately other members have your back...and you have theirs. And that there is an agreement, that as Commander Spock in *Star Trek* so eloquently said, "the needs of the many outweigh the needs of the few."

The principle of adaptive relationships has been in play for most of the organizations I've worked in from high-tech to fitness, where external partner relationships—and even internal cross-functional relationships—go through a continuous series of ebbs and flows. Where there is a clear sense of purpose and desired outcomes from the relationship—with a foundation of trust and the accountability of tracking tangible progress toward those mutually defined interests—partnerships not only endure they grow deeper over time.

Former Precor colleague **Jonathan Griffiths** is a veteran of building effective partnerships in the fitness and sporting event sponsorship space, and most recently in tech as VP Marketing–EMEA for managed service provider (MSP) Pax8 based in the UK. He agrees that alignment on objectives is critical in developing lasting, quality partnerships. But there are a few other major areas of shared commitment that make a huge difference.

The first is a shared focus on the customer.

"It's about taking a step back and going 'hang on, does this work for our particular buyer?' or 'do the people we want to partner with have our buyers in their audience mix that we want to get to'" If that works, it's a partnership meant to be. Like any relationship, it's got to work for both of you," Griffiths says.

The next is shared values, which have played out

very publicly in high-profile sports endeavors like FormulaOne with the banning of tobacco advertising, and even the Olympics where what is acceptable has changed from even several decades ago. He has a vivid, very personal example.

"My grandparents have a program for the 1948 Olympics with advertising for tobacco companies and industrial towns, which have fallen out of favor," he says.

At the end of the day, partnerships—especially those that are built through formal sponsorships—deliver the biggest impact when there is a clear route to new buying audiences, content co-creation creating engagement plus leads, and tangible measurement of relevant KPIs (SEO, tracking links to measure media channels and more).

Another dimension beyond partnerships is the relationship that companies form with their prospects and customers. This becomes especially critical in highly competitive technology markets where market noise is high and establishing differentiation requires separation in a sea of marketing clutter. Creating meaningful, lasting customer relationships is about so much more than bombarding them with messaging about product features and capabilities. It is about connection, about creating unique experiences. Most of all, it's about an expression of the values and reason of existence behind YOUR brand.

Apple and its legendary co-founder and CEO Steve Jobs knew this all too well.

In a famous video clip previewing the "Think Different"

campaign to an internal audience in the late 1990s, Jobs passionately talks about how while markets and competitors and products and distribution models can change, core values should never change. Building a breakthrough campaign with agency partner Chiat/Day only reinforced the realization that the Apple brand was about far more than as he put it "making boxes for people to get their jobs done." Its core value was, as Jobs put it, "people with passion can change the world for the better." And so this impactful campaign stayed true to that value by honoring courageous innovators, thought leaders, and artists celebrated by some, ridiculed or vilified by others including Albert Einstein, Thomas Edison, Amelia Earhardt, Gandhi, Muhammad Ali, Martin Luther King, and more.

So if understanding your core values and reason for being is fundamental in building authentic relationships with prospects and customers, having a well-thought-out, disciplined approach to engaging them is critical.

Marlowe Fenne, a member of my voice technology product management team at Active Voice and Cisco and now an Account Based Marketing (ABM) Director at Abnormal Security, has discovered that a more personalized approach to engaging prospects is the key to building stronger—and more profitable—relationships. This is all about better understanding the context of what your potential customer's pain points are.

"Personalization requires looking closely at what a customer's biggest challenges are, knowing what your specific capabilities are as a company, what the meaningful differentiation is, and how to hone it into something that is much more relevant to the customer based on the specific challenges they are going through," he says.

"What we're talking about is an 'audience of one' if you're doing great at it. It's about them instead of just the typical 'spray and pray' marketing that a lot of folks do," Fenne observes. "This is about taking your signal-to-noise ratio and amping it up, by driving into what will really resonate with that specific person, customer, or group of people who have a similar challenge they are trying to overcome."

This isn't about a bombardment of content. Twenty to twenty-five times higher response with ABM approaches that deliver more relevant messaging, with some of the most powerful coming in what Fenne calls a more "snackable" form.

Effectively managing prospect and customer communications is even more critical when separate organizations come together through mergers or acquisitions (M&A). This is the melding of unique cultures in a way that creates a positive, sustainable environment of high employee satisfaction and strong business performance. This is even more daunting when former competitors now become allies.

Joe Burton, CEO of Telesign, knows this all too well. In 2018 as CEO of Plantronics, he oversaw the $2 billion acquisition of Polycom and the creation of a new integrated company and brand called Poly.

This is reflective of a very active market over the past few years, with the estimated global value of M&A activity reaching a record of more than $5 trillion in 2021.

Having worked in and around a lot of technology acquisitions and integrations over more than two decades with a high-volume acquirer (Cisco), Burton knows just how challenging the process can be and is passionate about a fundamental question that needs to be answered to ensure success.

"The strategic rationale has to be right and enduring so this has to be good for the industry. It has to be a real problem that need to be solved, and can't be temporary," he says. "You've got to understand your strategy and understand what you're looking for."

Burton calls out a very useful analogy from our daily lives for the importance of pre-planning: grocery shopping.

"I tell people never go shopping when you're hungry. You're better off to sit at home. When you're not terribly hungry fill out the recipes you'd like to make for that week, build a shopping list then go to the store and go through that in a little more structured way" he suggests.

Even with the best-planned acquisitions that align strategically, bringing together two distinct cultures as seamlessly as possible is one of the toughest challenges the CEO of a new combined company will ever face. Often this means melding different sets of values during a process of great distraction for employees who may be distracted by organizational structure changes and a modification of corporate values. The level of commitment, of being "all in" on the new direction, can fluctuate across functions and teams. This is where leadership focuses on the human need for context and a reason to believe in the future to better process, commit, and move forward with action comes into play.

"In the case of Poly, we were bringing together a couple of companies because the industry was changing so we really had to continue the educational process on who both companies were before that world doesn't exist anymore," Burton recalls. "We've got to get ready for a new world. It's a bright future. It's a good one. But here's what that new world looks like and we've all got to be in it together."

One thing is certain: bringing together different companies with different companies requires discipline and patience.

"Culture change or culture melding is a long process," he says. "When I started this, we were told by culture experts this is a three to five-year journey if you're persistent to get the cultures to really come together."

Repetition, especially when it comes to informing employees, is crucial to keeping connected relationships during what is often a high-stress process.

"A lot of it really is to communicate, communicate and communicate what does the future look like, but also modeling the right behaviors. I had somebody tell me culture is like a guiding hand in the room that informs people what is ok to do, what is not ok to do even when the boss isn't there." Burton says.

Another powerful analogy related to bringing together different cultures and perspectives for the embracement of a shared company vision comes from the world of mountaineering.

Mark Pattison is Senior Vice President of Arena Group, a fast-growing publisher with an iconic brand lineup including *Sports Illustrated*. A former college football star at the University of Washington and member of the New Orleans Saints and Oakland Raiders in the NFL, he took on the audacious challenge—beginning at age 50—of scaling the tallest peak on every continent, now known as "The Seven Summits."

This challenge was first accomplished in 1985 by American climber Richard Bass—at the "advanced age" (in mountaineering terms) of 55.

The last of the peaks he needed to scale to meet his goal was Mount Everest, the tallest mountain in the world with a summit of over 29,000 feet. Just as in a larger scale M&A process, it takes months if not years of meticulous planning across a diverse team, from guides to sherpas to fellow climbers, often from different countries speaking different native languages and fighting volatile weather conditions to reach the Summit.

A long hard journey…but when it's accomplished as Pattison did in May 2021, at age 59, after nine years and having to re-do Denali in Alaska due to severe weather—and becoming one of less than 400 climbers to complete the Seven Summits and enduring a one-year COVID delay to conquer Everest, the collective excitement was indescribable.

Figure 2.4 Reaching the Summit of Everest

Courtesy: Mark Pattison

And as he reflects on his very long, at times unpredictable trip that resulted in reaching a magnificent goal, and his professional life overall, Pattison comes back to the power of focus, teamwork, and relationships as providing critical ignition to move from a concept to a successfully executed plan.

"Where your focus goes, your energy follows," he notes. And Pattison's energy was fueled as a football player under Hall of Fame coach Don James at Washington who grounded him in the principles of The Pyramid of Success, built by another legendary college coach John Wooden at UCLA. This is a life philosophy transcending athletics which was intended as a roadmap for being a better person. At the top of the pyramid is "Competitive Greatness", along with 24 other behavioral characteristics. The foundational base of the pyramid features key attributes to relationships, including friendship, loyalty, and cooperation.

Figure 2.5 John Wooden Pyramid of Success

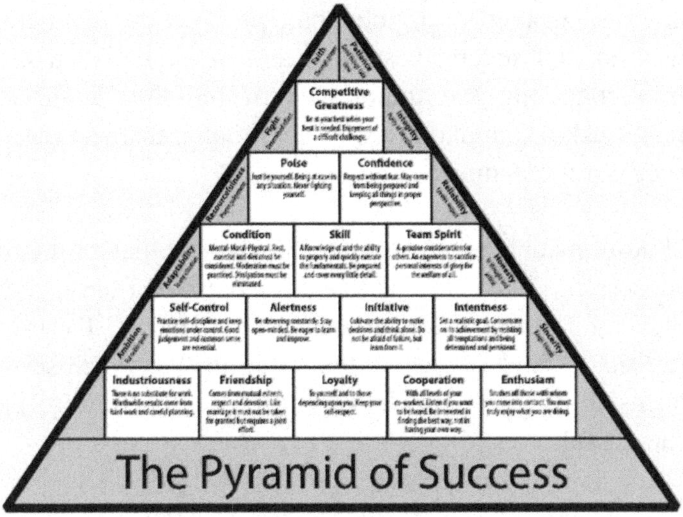

Courtesy: John Wooden Institute

Pattison applied the concepts of the Pyramid to nurturing several key relationships that both inspired and transformed his life and helped him through all of the highs—and lows that come with pursuing your dreams.

"One of the things we all experience, it doesn't matter who you are whether you're an athlete or a mountain climber or anything like that. It's all about how we capture momentum and then momentum sometimes stops. And the question is how you recapture that and keep it going," he says.

Pattison gained perspective and confidence through relationships developed with several other accomplished climbers including Ed Visteurs (one of less than 50 people who climbed all 14 8,000-meter peaks, and he did it without using supplemental oxygen!). I had the opportunity to get to know Visteurs in recruiting him as a keynote speaker for a global partner event my company was hosting several years ago and he echoed Pattison in recognizing the importance of building a strong relationship foundation across a climbing team to reach successful outcomes.

"I don't just have one person, I find people that have had success and it's a little bit like a franchise in a sense, and they figured out a way to stamp and repeat," Pattison reflects. "And so there's the value in the franchise in terms of all that knowledge and power on how to be successful."

Beyond internal teams and across organizations, there is an even bigger opportunity to build healthy, lasting relationships with the Communities where we live—a way to partner and give back as socially responsible members of your community at large.

TJ Fox, Senior Vice President of Industrial IoT and Automotive at Verizon, a leading global telecommunications provider, has witnessed the power of connecting and relationship building with local communities.

When the COVID pandemic exploded it started having a sweeping impact on everyone from students to working families to small business owners to global businesses, some deep company values quickly rose to the surface.

"Part of our culture is we live in communities in which we serve and we serve those," Fox says. "We have an obligation and society is one of our four stakeholders and they're equal stakeholders."

Examples of Verizon efforts include partnering with small businesses in providing for, and distributing more than 80,000 meals front line health care workers in New York City, expanding that program to Detroit with the help of the Ford Motor Company, and weekly "pay it forward" streaming events with major music and game entertainment carried on all its platforms and pledging millions of dollars in small business grants across the U.S. to keep these local owners afloat during times of lockdown and unpredictable customer traffic.

Verizon also built a stronger relationship with small and medium businesses through a free webinar series reaching thousands with advice on everything from available loan programs and other available best practice tools and services.

"Leadership is easy when skies are blue and you know you've got fair winds and smooth seas. Where leadership really matters is when it's stormy outside" Fox says.

With some of their surveys showing almost 50% of small businesses projecting they'll unlikely need to have smaller staffs and close to 70% saying they can recoup losses incurred during COVID, the outlook is improving.

"These are the kind of things that should give us all a lot

of confidence," he adds. "And I'm very confident about the technologies on how to assist them in these kind of stormy waters."

TAKEAWAYS CHECKLIST:

☑ Recognize your place as part of a broader "human ecosystem" where being intentional and proactive opens the door for meaningful relationships

☑ Bring an adaptive, flexible and empathetic attitude along with a commitment to being fully "present" in all your customer, team member, partner, networking, and community relationships

☑ Accept that the melding of a different company or team members' cultures, processes, and values takes time and in times of great change and uncertainty, leadership clarity on context and the desired future state makes all the difference

3

DIVERSE VOICES

---

di·ver·si·ty – *the practice or quality of including or involving people from a range of different social and ethnic backgrounds and of different genders, sexual orientations, etc.*

In a world raging with conflict, and with many fearful of conflict, the late author Audre Lorde made a great observation when she noted, "It is not our differences that divide us. It is our inability to recognize, accept, and celebrate those differences."

An organization that fails to enable, and hear, a diversity of voices is like preparing a multi-course meal using two ingredients. Sure, you might be able to fill a plate but without utilizing a full range of ingredients that provide richness, texture, and spice the resulting taste experience hardly pleases the palate.

One of the greatest personal gifts I have received through my leadership experience in global companies of all different shapes, sizes, and industries is gaining an authentic appreciation for the positive impacts of advocating, and cultivating, diversity—of age, gender, language, race, sexual orientation, work/life experiences, and much more. It's one thing to advocate through words.

Where the "rubber hits the road "ultimately is embracing it, committing to it, and living it every day.

The importance of having a kaleidoscope of perspectives, to see things through a diversity of lenses that replicate the spectrum of humans in the markets you serve to thrive as an organization is well documented. And a popular perception these days is that businesses "have come a long way" in embracing diversity in their hiring, promotions and general workplace practices. Just how far?

Julie Dexter Berg, Chief Marketing Office of security solutions provider Privoro and a highly accomplished marketing leader for multi-billion-dollar companies from retail to wireless, has a cringe-worthy memory of her early days as a consumer-packaged goods marketer for Carnation.

"When I first started in the 1980s the executive floor did not have a ladies' room, only a men's room," she recalls. "So, if you were in a meeting on the executive floor, you had to go down to the seventh floor to use the restroom."

After Carnation's sale to Nestlè, things did not get much better.

"Nestlè was a Swiss company, very male-dominated. I actually was in a meeting, presenting, and I had these Swiss Nestlè guys ask me to go get the coffee. Stunning. There were just two of us that were women leaders, director-level types. You know we sort of laughed but it was also just shocking."

Her time with USWest was refreshing in that the company put a high premium on diversity and inclusion, evolving their recruiting process to ensure that every slate of candidates for open positions. I worked in her organization as it merged into the AirTouch Wireless business, and was inspired by her dynamic, engaging communication style.

But later in her career, when leading large Marketing teams for SuperValue, Cricket Wireless and even at her current job, Dexter Berg again found herself one of the very few women on the executive team. But there is hope.

Committing to diversification in recruiting is a big first step. She is encouraged by some larger companies that are making inroads on more than just gender.

"Many large companies like Microsoft and Dell and Chevron to name have specific recruiting strategies around neurodiversity. Essentially, it's the umbrella term for people who are on the autistic spectrum, ADHD, and so forth that have been largely overlooked by traditional hiring and recruiting strategies," Dexter Berg says.

While working a traditional "in-person" schedule and interacting with others in office settings is challenging, the emergence of remote work has enabled the discovery of unique talents.

"They have really interesting skills around focus pattern recognition. They bring a lot of interesting skills to certain kinds of jobs. This is a new sort of pocket in the workforce that have been overlooked but should be included where appropriate," Dexter Berg points out. But to demonstrate unique skills, diverse candidates need to be actively sourced and as part of a very intentional diversity recruiting strategy.

Karyn Scott, a senior marketing leader at several prominent technology providers including Cisco and Salesforce, sees diversity as mission-critical to effectively recruiting and retaining employees—especially the next generation of workers—given that employers are riding out the bubble of diversity as one of their cornerstone strategies.

"Because social media is so prevalent and everybody and everything is connected in real-time, I see a lot of business leaders thinking about how to create that environment in my business, in my DNA, in my value system because it's going to be a differentiator when you think about retaining top talent and recruiting the next generation," she says.

"I have kids in their twenties, and they would never think of working for a company that doesn't have very strong ethics around diversity, equity, and inclusion."

Yvan Demosthenes, CEO of HamiltonDemo, a national recruiting firm, has been a tireless advocate for an "all in" diversity recruiting strategy for more than a decade. One of the most critical steps he advises that leaders take in ensuring successful recruiting outcomes is achieving common ground on the definition of diversity.

"I've been in many board rooms, and someone will say 'diversity' and then I'll say, 'if we go around the room,

I bet you will have different views and ideas on what diversity is' and that's what happens," Demosthenes shares.

Beyond level-setting your teams on what your organization's diversity objectives are, he sees it often comes down to having a mindset that is open to new approaches.

"Whether you've been intentional or not, if you're not getting the results, maybe it's time to change. Maybe it's time to mix things up. It's the old story: you know you can't keep fishing in the same pond and expect to catch different fish."

Embracing diversity and committing to action is a big part of the equation but trying to simplify it down to a single approach will not be a panacea for all the ills in a company. Demosthenes cautions leaders to have realistic expectations for the effort that will be required.

"I've never seen a magic pill to remedy an organization that's looking for an impactful diversity recruiting strategy," he says. "You're usually attracting smaller populations of people. A lot of organizations also think that if they do the right thing, the floodgates are going to open. I would caution against that. If you do a great job, maybe anticipate a heavy stream or consistent drip. Things will come, you'll fill that bucket."

Failing to create a diverse environment that shapes your culture can have a massive negative impact on your effectiveness in achieving a meaningful connection with key internal stakeholders (who you work with regularly) and external audiences (your customers).

My own experience at global companies including Cisco, Honeywell, and Precor revealed an "inside-out" truth: embracing and leveraging diverse backgrounds and perspectives from your internal teams is a critical pre-requisite to effectively developing external-facing, targeted marketing strategies that will engage diverse customers.

Elisabeth Kurek, Vice President of Marketing at IONOS, a leading web-hoster, is a world traveler who has immersed herself in different countries through work and personal journeys that have sharpened her appreciation of diverse cultures and business approaches.

As an American based outside of the United States, Kurek knows the necessity of collaboratively working with very diverse global teams. This means doing a bit of basic homework upfront to better understand cultural nuances and the little things that could make a big impact in working better together.

"So, if you're working with a team in another region where you might not know the culture directly, just take a few minutes and try to learn about it or where you can learn from other colleagues on a micro level," she suggests.

Kurek recalls getting small bits of advice from some colleagues when based in Florida working for a Japanese-owned company. Given the more formal tone customary in Japan, doing the very simple thing of adding a "-son" next to the names she was writing emails to was recognized as an act of respect.

Email can be a tricky form of business communication, made even more complicated when exchanges involve non-native language use. Without the benefit of physical cues or tone of voice, the intent of countless emails is misinterpreted. She recalls one awkward example involving a Marketing colleague based in Germany where an email to a U.S.-based sales leader resulted in unnecessary tension.

"The sales manager came over said 'What is going on with this marketing manager in Germany, this is so rude I can't believe she sent this!'" After Kurek looked at the actual email, she realized the sender was trying to say the topic was very urgent. But in the translation that got lost and came across to the recipient as rude. Ultimately the two parties to this worked through it with the Sales manager learning a valuable lesson.

"Even if something comes in and you think 'wow that sounded rude or that was abrupt or the person didn't answer my question', just take a few minutes to think about what was behind it and ask before you assume what the person's intent was. It's not possible to every nuance of every culture in the world. So just take a few minutes to think, 'okay, what did that person really mean?'"

Figure 3.1 Multilingual World

Another valuable learning experience came from her team meetings, wherein a group setting her Japanese colleagues would be reluctant to ask questions following one of her marketing or technical presentations.

"I would ask 'does anyone have any questions, does everyone understand?' So, silence and I learned that within the Japanese culture people would not speak up on the phone. With the different teams I would ask just one on one 'did you have any questions about that, did you want me to take a few extra minutes and give you a quick follow-up call to explain the last section?' Usually the answer was yes."

Rachelle Franklin, a former classmate of mine at the McCombs Graduate School of Business at the University of Texas at Austin, is a dynamic marketing leader who has been an impact maker at major brands including Motorola, Office Depot and Cable and Wireless. She is the founder and CEO of Frontline Marketing & Promotions which helps major brands such as Microsoft better reach diverse audiences through online marketing, social media, mobile outreach and experiential marketing.

Reaching highly diverse audiences with a resonating, relevant message requires a crisp, clear reason for being and having a comprehensive understanding of who you are communicating with.

"One thing that became clear after I had done all those years at Motorola and into a number of different enterprises and now as an entrepreneur is there are some things that are true as a marketer," she says. "No matter the industry, if you know your customer, truly deeply and intimately and you segment your market you're going to have a better chance of succeeding despite where you are in business—be it a startup or a mature enterprise."

It seems so obvious. Know your customer, develop relevant messaging and reach them in the communication channels where they reside. But most companies discover becoming more customer-centric is never as easy as it seems on paper.

"Some of the biggest obstacles are they're so busy running the business and growing the business and trying to develop products and bring them to market that they don't think about the customer," Franklin says.

Franklin recommends her clients use a straightforward technique to assess how customer-focused their organizations are.

"One of the litmus tests is when you sit in a meeting, how many times are you talking about the customer? How often is the customer in the conversation? If you really sit back and think about it and are really conscious of it, you'll find that a lot of meetings internally are more about operations," she observes. "Is the customer front and center to the decisions that you're making about your business?"

The value of getting to know and appreciate the diversity of your customers is not merely a truth for technology companies. There are plenty of compelling examples in other more mature, traditional categories such as food and beverage.

Wiley Mullins is a marketer at heart, honing his craft as consumer-packaged goods giants Procter & Gamble and Cadbury Schweppes. When he recruited me to join his team early in my career I was inspired by his creativity, positive energy and always striving to problem-solve with a diverse perspective.

Making a big leap to an entrepreneur by founding Uncle Wiley's Specialty Foods nearly 30 years ago, Mullins nurtures and promotes healthy eating by producing "Healthy Southern Classics" seasonings and spices (built from his passion for southern foods and a base of his grandmother's recipes) has been nothing short of transformational. Gaining and maintaining distribution in major national grocery chains, competing with established brands, and spending millions more dollars on marketing, were made possible by a relentless focus on the needs of his diverse customers.

Traditional positioning statements include a definition of the target audience, your frame of reference, and your point of difference. But Mullins needed to position his products more diversely than narrowly.

"Early on we created what we feel like was a positioning statement that was narrow enough but yet broader enough to really reach out to several consumer segments," he says.

"Our primary target audience is southerners who like southern ethnic foods. Secondarily, would be health-conscious people who ware wanting to eat more natural but don't know how to prepare the foods like collards or turnip greens, so we have seasonings that allow them to."

Of course, thinking more broadly does not mean sacrificing having a distinct reason for being.

"Really focus on something you can be known for. It's somewhat flattering when you have other people that want to take your ideas and develop them so I would tell people instead of trying to be all things to all people, identify something you can just zone in on and you can blow it up from right there."

Leadership perspectives on diversity are no doubt shaped by the very personal—and at times challenging—experiences in their journey.

Stephanie Carhee, Founder and President of UC Interlink, successfully competes with bigger competitors with bigger budgets in consulting with a wide range of Fortune 500 companies on the successful adoption of emerging advanced technologies. Carhee is a self-made success story. Her entry into the technology space was not the result of a highly pre-meditated plan. There was a time she wasn't that passionate about technology, her heart was in journalism. But a persistent recruiter convinced her to keep an open mind and ultimately, for more than a decade, she made a difference in helping drive the rapid growth of new Cisco telephony and unified communications technologies around the world.

As a company founder in the technology space, and as a woman of color, Carhee realizes she is in a very unique situation.

"Working in technology, let's be honest, there's just not a lot of people of color that do what we do and it's not because the skillset isn't there. It's because you just don't get the opportunity to do that," she reflects.

By not creating more of these opportunities, companies miss a chance to generate even more breakthrough ideas.

"The innovation and the ingenuity of being able to do something even better comes from bringing in outside voices that are not like you and so it was disheartening to me the hundreds and hundreds of customers I've had a chance to interact with, I would be in the room with CEOs of some of the top companies and I would look around the room and there was no one that looks like me," Carhee says.

With all the social upheaval and increased recent attention to diversity, equity, and inclusion, Carhee sees a crack in the door for meaningful progress.

"During this culture shift that we're having as a country, and as the world is changing, let's all try and embrace each other in a way that would allow for us to take advantage of the fact that there are voices beyond our own that could bring amazing experiences," she suggests. "As humans, we're creatures of habit, we like to do what we're comfortable with, and sometimes being uncomfortable is a chance where you get an amazing opportunity that maybe you wouldn't have had before."

A huge, and very visible, measuring stick for progress in the inclusion of diverse voices is looking at representation within corporate leadership. And while it is generally acknowledged that we are moving in a positive direction from a DEI perspective, clearly a lot more work needs to be done. A Gartner Leadership Survey shows while women make up 56 percent of front-line employees, they only represent 29 percent of the C-suite.

Board of Director composition tells a similar story, with ISS Corporate Solutions Data showing while growing, with underrepresented groups accounting for only 17 percent of seats, and women representing only 27 percent.

Having more gender, racial and experiential diversity in the C-suite isn't always just about structural barriers put in place by organizations or the narrow mindset of other decision makers who are making hiring or promotion decisions. Sometimes it can be blocked or delayed by a self-imposed mindset, a lack of belief in what is possible, from those who are the most deserving.

Cathy Yang, Chief Financial Officer of C&K Switches, with annual sales in excess of $200 million, is a case in point.

She was my finance business partner at Intermec (later acquired by Honeywell), and I knew she was destined for great things in her career. It wasn't just her financial acumen (honed by a steady progression of experience at ConocoPhillips and in subsequent corporate FP&A plus global channel business roles), but her collaborative approach to looking outside the numbers and seeing things from a broader business strategy perspective. I always got a strong sense this was in the spirit of making the best investment decisions for the organization and I appreciated her openness, honesty, and constructive counsel.

Having grown up in Taiwan, coming to the United States, and earning her MBA at Purdue, she observed some major gaps early in her career.

"When I started off, I worked in a very professional environment in large corporations, and I was learning a lot of the job and I was surrounded by very smart and very successful leaders," Yang recalls. "But at that point I felt one thing was missing. The company was very keen in driving diversity, but I did not see any female at the executive table and of course no Asian female because it was not quite there yet."

Despite her academic and professional accomplishments

in reaching the C-suite of a nine-figure global business, Yang admits her career trajectory was challenged by a sense of modesty and a lack of confidence. But she was able to overcome those doubts to achieve professional success.

"I was raised in a Chinese culture where my mom and dad always told me to be very modest and modesty is considered a virtue so when I accomplished something I always thought that is what I should do and that is nothing to be celebrated about and its' just a given," she says. "I always wanted to look at things from a couple of different perspectives, but I never thought that my voice should or can be heard loudly and that's what you would call personal ceiling. But there's always this little voice inside me saying 'why not?' and that is a voice that kept me going with my journey."

Yang is appreciative of the encouragement she has received from various senior Finance leaders during earlier stages of her career, including sharing advice for her personal growth or informing her of new opportunities. In one case, it was an executive who told her directly he wanted to help "unlock her potential" which resulted in her taking on roles that moved her closer to the functional lines of business, including Channel Sales, Engineering, and Marketing.

Being grateful for the support–and impact–of others, Yang is very motivated to help the next generation of diverse voices be heard by setting a positive example for others and by giving back through mentorship.

"I've always told myself I need to keep that in mind so

that I'm paying forward, and I love mentoring people again," she says. "No official programs, but if somebody comes to me, I'm willing and open to share with them my experiences. Right or wrong, success or failure. I do believe by sharing we're shaping this next generation of leaders in the place where they care about their jobs."

Another passionate advocate for mentoring is **Bridget Bisnette**, who for nearly four decades has driven channel sales and marketing impact, including leading large teams at Cisco and Riverbed Technologies.

In Bisnette's case, reaching the highest levels of leadership in technology companies was not the result of a formal, grand plan when she entered the professional working world. After getting an entry-level job at AST computers, she was driven by her curiosity and boldness in trying new things. Even in the absence of formal training, she spent a lot of time in manufacturing groups and with the engineering team during the era of what she describes as an "if we build it, they will come" model.

From there her additional years at Cisco developing certification programs put her on the map for enabling channel partners in entirely new ways.

But even as she took on progressively more senior roles, Bisnette was navigating a very delicate balancing act between career and personal life. There was a self-realization that the way she approached work might need to be a bit different from what her male colleagues did.

"The number one challenge I faced every single day and being in this industry is balancing my family responsibilities with my work responsibilities and when you have to do that, there's tradeoffs and the tradeoffs happen," Bisnette says.

"You know every year you just have to decide where you're going to invest your time. And in order for me to get as much as I can out of both those aspects of my life, I have to be very focused and very efficient. I don't want to say it's a male thing because I think it's just a work thing."

Bisnette remembers her prioritizing balance of family life earlier in her career requiring opting out of the outside of work network and relationship-building that was more common with her male colleagues.

"I just knew I couldn't work like the guys worked, it wasn't an option for me, so I had to work my way and be as impactful as possible. And my style as a female leader is very consistent and grounded on what I talk about with the partners and that is I always try to focus on what's right for the customer and not necessarily what's right for my peers or politically correct. I am very results-oriented, I am very driven and some of that comes from the fact I have to focus in order to get all these other aspects of my life fit in the 24 hours we have."

Figure 3.2 Meritocracia

Bisnette is grateful for having so many strong females in her life and has grown herself from sharing her journey and perspectives with other women advancing their careers.

"I have had the pleasure of working in and around so many women in my life and the greatest result for me is kind of like what you might say about a teacher when I run into someone and they're like 'you were the best boss I ever had' or 'you know I'm the leader I am today because you mentored me and you coached me.' That's just so rewarding."

Mentoring other women have a special plate in the heart for **Sue Taylor**, a veteran of the C-suite in serving as the Chief Information Officer for the Bill and Melinda Gates Foundation which is fighting poverty, disease, and inequity around the world. Her experience there and in other technology companies sharpened both her appreciation for gender representation gaps and the huge influence on behaviors that merely establishing a clear improvement goal can bring.

"It's a sad state for us to sit here and talk about the fact that the pipeline of girls and young women entering technology fields has not improved over the past decade," she laments. "What do we do to change that? How do we make it a much more inclusive organization and support young girls and women? At the Foundation we made a management that we would increase diversity within our workforce and over four years our technology team is almost fifty-fifty gender mix and that is almost a 28 percent increase in gender diversity."

Taylor is also proud of her team's sponsorship of Ignite, an organization supporting young girls from middle school through high school, and has leaders from the Foundation speak to them about different opportunities in STEM. She is also very active in the growing community called Women of the Pacific Northwest, a group of around 30 women IT leaders in Oregon and Washington that actively mentor and support each other. This is on top of connecting with other female CIOs through conferences and speaking panels.

"What I have discovered with this network of women leaders is how many insightful leaders we have in the country," she says. "We think about change management, culture, and organization dynamics in addition to the technology piece of it."

No doubt diversity thrives more in organizations when leaders "pay it forward" by helping others by sharing their unique experiences via mentoring or helping open doors for the underrepresented that might not ever have been open before. At the end of the day, embracing diversity means rejecting sameness, celebrating the differences in the human race, and a commitment to continuous learning—sometimes getting comfortable with the uncomfortable.

Phyllis Turner-Brim has made it a personal goal to do all she can to improve racial diversity in her field of patent law. Her time and philanthropy are increasingly focused on the area of diversity, equity, and inclusion. She's very intentional in sharing her story.

"Nobody expects the chief IP counsel of HP to be a black woman. They don't expect it to be me. People didn't expect the chief IP counsel of Intellectual Ventures would be a black woman. It led to some very interesting circumstances when things that would be discussed in ways people would be treated and ways I would be treated before they knew who I was," she says. "That's a very sad commentary."

On the flip side, Turner-Brim is encouraged there is increased focus on diversity, equity, and inclusion, where research consistently shows companies make more money and get better overall business results when their teams are diverse.

"People interested in better outcomes must be more interested in diversity," she says.

Turner-Brim also encourages people to focus on what she calls the "technology gap." This requires an investment in lower grade levels to get minorities and girls interested in STEM so they can hit the field of IP law fully credentialed.

When the traditional thinking of work teams—even very technical teams—is challenged by blending in people who bring very diverse life and work experiences, incredible outcomes happen.

Dillana Lim, CEO of Versium, a marketing audience, and targeting platform, became a high-impact player in advanced technology teams relatively early in her career, even without a formal technical background.

Fueled by a deep passion for technology, she created value by serving as a strategic translator of sorts, a human bridge between highly technical engineers and non-technical business strategists.

"I could translate what they needed to the business, and I could also translate what the business needs to the developers and that early trust that was built between me and my different teams is really the basis for a lot of my career success", Lim says.

"I always found teams I enjoyed working with, products that I felt really needed to see a place in the market and the development teams helped me bridge any technology gap. As long as you're willing to listen and learn, as long as you understand and really love working in technology, it's very easy to move your way up without a formal background."

Beyond her personal experience, Lim feels some of the

strongest technologists that she works with also do not have formal technology backgrounds. What made this possible?

"Their passion was the thing that made up for it and you can see it, what they produce and what they work on."

Another factor that makes diversity of background work well—and build trust—in highly technical organizations is making smart choices in *how* to communicate. Delivering simpler, more direct communication pays off.

"Engineers do not respond well to a lot of business vernacular, because it changes every ten years," she observes. "What they really want to know is what are the things that they will build that will get in the most hands and solve the most problems."

Her passion for developing a culture built on diversity as the most senior leader in her organization is also driven by her customer focus.

"Our customers are diverse, and so we need a level of diversity when it comes to making decisions about what our customers need," she says. "One of the things that is different now versus when I started my career is that the definition of diversity has changed. When I started, it was just to get a woman a seat at the table. Everyone would give themselves accolades for that. But now, I think everyone understands that diversity and means a lot more than just one aspect of a person, it means a diversity of experiences, backgrounds, education, and ages."

Better reflecting on your customers at all levels of the organization not only produces better outcomes and perspectives but also drives greater efficiency.

"You're able to identify issues quicker because you actually have someone from a different experience or background helping you make those decisions' admits Lim. "It can't be a secondary thought; it has to be something that you think about when you're making a decision."

Lim cites the Nasdaq requirement for women to be on the board of companies it publicly lists as a great example of keeping diversity front and center as a priority.

There's another truth in all of this. Making diversity real across your entire organization also means recognizing the potential for stirring up internal conflict and seeing the positive aspects of constructive debate.

"When you broaden that diversity of perspective and opinions, that means there are going to be disagreements and so there has to be the willingness to see the positive aspects of a healthy conflict. Getting to the right outcome sometimes can be a little daunting. But everything always ends up better when people feel free to speak their mind on their proposed solution. Not everybody's idea will be incorporated, but everybody will be heard."

Beyond the walls of your organization lies a bigger opportunity to show relevance through social responsibility. This impacts everything from recruiting and developing human capital to the market perception of brands, and it has only grown in profile over the past two decades. Lim knows all too well the "table stakes" have changed.

"The role of the corporation has also shifted within the last twenty years," she says. "It used to be very much focused on serving shareholders. That was what you learned in business school and now people have said 'wait a second, that's not fully true,'" she says.

"The corporation doesn't just serve shareholders it serves customers, employees, and the economy. It also makes an impact on the climate. Shareholders expect companies to have other programs in place to build goodwill."

With plenty of media coverage still devoted to exposing bad business behaviors and the negative impact of climate change, it is encouraging to see increasing examples of large, global companies like Amazon making progress on things from elevating minimum wage to reducing their carbon footprint.

This increased focus on social responsibility has come hand in hand with some steady progress on increasing diversity representation on corporate Boards. According to the Alliance for Board Diversity (ABD), the number of Fortune 500 companies with over 40% diversity representation on their boards is nearly four times higher than it was in 2010. A bit more sobering is it may take as much as fifty more years to reach its aspirational goal of 40% of companies hitting this standard.

Janis Harwell is a seasoned business and legal executive, serving as a Senior Vice President at Intermec and Monsanto, and Pacific Telesis Group. She has served on several boards, including Delta Dental of Washington and the Northwest African American Museum.

In our highly disrupted and dynamic world, Harwell sees three main ingredients as the "table steaks" for companies and their Boards to have a shot at being great. And the first is embracing Diversity.

"First you need a mix of skill sets at the Board level, a mix of experience, capabilities, and demographic profiles. Second, every effort has to be made needs to foster a climate of mutual respect and sympathetic listening so that Directors and management can benefit from the diverse perspectives on the Board," she says. "Otherwise, you get things like complacency, overconfidence, myopia, and groupthink, any one of those can be fatal to the company."

According to Harwell, the benefits of fresh perspectives are especially amplified when a Board is infused with younger members that have different experiences and bring a vision of the future that may be more accurate.

A final, and very critical, factor in great Boards according to Harwell is the recognition by Directors that the companies they serve don't exist as a silo. They are part of a vast ecosystem called society.

Figure 3.3 Non-diverse Board

**"Today's theme is
'Getting Beyond Group Think."**

"Pretending that a business exists in a vacuum can have devastating effects on the lives, livelihoods, and liberty of many human beings within and outside of the company. Serious efforts have to be made to keep the cascade effects of corporate behavior in view at the Board level so that it can try to prevent disastrous outcomes."

While the path to being great by executing on these dimensions seems straightforward, reality says differently. Diversity has been a very tough nut to crack, due in part to challenges associated with managing Board transitions, especially the preparation and onboarding of new Directors, who may not be fully ready for their new responsibilities.

"It's difficult to take yourself out of what you already know. Everyone will go through time when they accidentally fall back into the lawyer thing, the CEO thing, the marketing thing, whatever you were doing before," she says. "There's a lot of anxiety in picking somebody that cannot make the transition to being a director from whatever they were doing before. Like any small team, trying to get to the place where you develop the relationships, trust the confidence and the respect it takes for a team to work well together. It's a process. Not all Boards or candidates have the attitudes they need to make sure the onboarding of new Directors is successful."

The bottom line is that voluntary diversification efforts have not worked. The failure of these efforts has resulted in federal and state laws, along with shareholder demands for companies to achieve specific diversification targets within specific timeframes. But even with these in place, ultimate success still boils down to having the most senior leaders fully bought in.

"We can expect these efforts will reduce poor results unless the Chairman of the Board and CEO are committed to meaningful diversification of the Board," she says. "These individuals have huge influence over the nomination and selection process. If they're not with the program of diversity you get either no success, you miss your goals completely, or you get tokenistic solutions, like one woman on a fourteen-person board or one minority on a fourteen-person board. All the studies show that you need critical mass when you're diversifying. It's roughly at least three of whatever new type of person you're bringing on. And the reason is that it's really easy for one or two people who are different from the rest of the Board to feel isolated and ignored or be treated as a wildcard that's on the fringe of the process."

TAKEAWAYS CHECKLIST:

☑ Achieving diversity that is equitable and inclusive includes not just being open to a more gender and racial-diverse employee base, it includes the representation of a wide range of professional experiences and team members at different career maturity stages

☑ Understanding the diverse nature of your customer base and their unique needs, then reflecting it in your customer messaging is a key to achieving meaningful connection and long-term customer loyalty

☑ Board diversification ultimately will succeed— or fail—based on the personal commitment and advocacy of the Chairman of the Board and CEO and needs to aim for "critical mass" in the placement of under-represented groups

MEET THE IMPACT MAKERS

Michelle
Accardi

Bridget
Bisnette

Karen
Bissani

Laura
Blackmer

Donnie
Boivin

Steve
Brossman

Peter
Burghardt

Joe Burton

Pat Byrne

Stephanie
Carhee

Alan Cohen

Alison Conigliaro-
Hubbard

Lori Cooper
Wolfe

Ross Daniels

Sandeep Dayal

Marthin
De Beer

Christi
DeCuir

Yvan
Demosthenes

Julie Dexter Berg

Marlowe
Fenne

John
Flannery

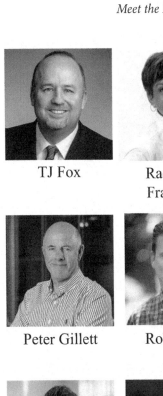

TJ Fox

Rachelle
Franklin

Ben Gibson

Peter Gillett

Rob Grady

Paul Green

Jonathan
Griffiths

Steve
Gutzler

Brianna
Haag

Art Harding

Janis
Harwell

Phillip
Hunter

Barry
Issberner

Lisa Jasper

Elisabeth
Kurek

Jim Liggett

Dillana Lim

Chris
Litherland

Michael Litt

Stephynie
Malik

Jordan
McCann

Dan McGaw

Darshan
Mehta

Joli Mosier

Wiley
Mullins

Ken Myer

Sushila
Nair

Sarah Nicastro

Tim Parkin

Mark
Pattison

Steve
Prentice

Billy Price

Don Proctor

Firaas
Rashid

Steve
Reasner

Sharon Richardson
Howell

Nancy Ridge

Kathryn
Robinson

Megan
Roudebush

Clive
Sawkins

Matthew
Schmidt

Eli Schwartz

Karyn Scott

Peter
Shafer

Jonathan
Shroyer

Keri Smith

Scott Smith

Karthik
Suresh

Kory
Tarpenning

Sue Taylor

Dan Thurmon

William
Toll

John
Traynor

Troy
Trenchard

Phyllis
Turner-Brim

Vijay
Velamoor

Jamison
West

Mike Wills

Asheligh
Wilson

Cathy Yang

Kristin
Zhivago

Notes

Data, Data, Data

---

da·ta – *facts and statistics collected together for reference or analysis*

In our complex business world where meaningful innovations are made, trusted relationships are built and diverse perspectives are valued, there has never been a time in human history where more raw data is available and collected to inform decisions.

Researchers from the University of Portsmouth (UK) estimate the amount of data created, captured, copied, and consumed in the world will reach a jaw-dropping 175 million zettabytes (zm) by 2025, with one zettabyte equaling 8,000,000,000,000,000,000,000 bits.

Leaders and teams in all functions, from product to finance to human resources to operations to marketing to sales, are inundated with quantitative and qualitative information about prospects, customers, costs, revenue, profit, customers, partners, and more.

This explosion in data volume is closely linked to advances in how it is referenced for multi-generational reverence. Since the first cave paintings some 40,000 years ago, printed books more than 1,500 years ago, and the beginnings of digital transformation in the mid-20th century with the invention of the transistor and integrated microchips, the form factors of consumption have continuously evolved to enable more and more intake.

With an abundance of seemingly infinitely scalable storage solutions, humans are swimming in a sea of information that has the potential to drown just as much as it supports bold new explorations. The question facing leaders isn't a question of *availability*, it's around effective, safe *interpretation*, and efficient *application*.

One of the most critical areas for any growing business, especially very young ones, on making smart data decisions on how to interact with audiences in the sales process.

Steve Brossman is a former professional track athlete in Australia and the founder of several six- and seven-figure global businesses, including an environmental product selling more than four million units across 16 countries. He has trained more than 65,000 business owners on how to stand out in their markets and excel in virtual selling.

Merely loading up prospects and customers with a ton of data in a corporate sales deck in the hopes of helping them make an "informed decision", is a recipe for failure. He points out that effectively presenting in the sales process in a world where video communication is even more of a norm is a bit of an art and a science.

"The art is the art of communication. We live in the

world of Zoomtopia. It's a different art and skill and flow of communication to be able to do it in front of a camera. 55% of communication is body language, now it's squeezed into a box," Brossman says.

"We have to learn to use our body language and our tonality, intonation, and cadence to keep them engaged. The science is people on video calls, it was 66% now it's 83% of people are multitasking. You've got to be more compelling and deliver your presentation that will keep their attention. Science says the more they are engaged in the actual decision-making and the presentation, the more likely they are to buy. We teach people to collaborate with them, agree on a value-based outcome and quantify that outcome. When they're collaborating, they're involved. When they're involved, they invest."

Interaction is key. Brossman advocates using a blueprint versus a generic set of slideware, and questions that come up dictate where you start which allows for real-time annotation on the screen that creates a more personalized experience and people in the virtual meeting are building it together versus a regurgitation of the same thing the previous person saw before.

"When we work around a blueprint and we're actually annotating, the questions come up first to direct where on the blueprint you start, where you go, and what you do," he says.

"You never do the same one twice whereas if you've got a slide deck people will be sitting down knowing that the person before them saw exactly the same. When you're working with the modern blueprint writing out or annotating the numbers then it's an individualized presentation specifically for them and they're leaning in they're thinking we're building this together. The science has basically shown that when you annotate and like draw on a screen with people, attention and knowledge retention go up sixty percent and their engaged engagement goes up sixty percent as well. But action at the end goes up eight times."

Data is not only vital in building healthy direct sales relationships; it is also absolutely critical for achieving maximum results through channel partner relationships.

Karen Bissani is one of the most exceptional marketing leaders I've had the privilege of managing, and after more than fifteen years at Cisco has gone on to propel marketing excellence at Veritas and Infoblox. She has seen first-hand the power of data extending across the entire spectrum of direct and indirect sales channels.

"When you talk about working with your sales teams as well as your channel partners, the other thing that comes into play is making sure you have the right data," she recommends. "Many companies consider who they are going to target, who are their customers. In some of the larger companies I've worked in we had the benefit of having our own data to get to the right decision makers. But I've also been in companies where we didn't have that data and one of the things, I wish we would have done more of is really making the investment needed to get the right data to make sure our programs are targeting the right customers. This also has to do with getting the right data to work together and through your channel partners."

Generating demand, and creating engagement and action is an art, a science, and also a data-informed process that even with advances in technology never diminishes the importance of understanding customer needs.

Art Harding, Chief Operating Officer at people.ai, has been a revenue driver for more than two decades in several successful technology companies including Vertias, Symantec, VMWare, and Riverbed Technology. He sees intelligent use of data as absolutely critical for effectively engaging in the buyer and customer journey. Instead of digital transformation and ai-assisted, data-driven modernization, Harding sees successful growth strategies as being more driven by a customer-focused process.

"Too often people make the mistake that these modernizations are actually technology-driven and I have a different point of view. I think these transformations are driven by new ways of thinking to re-engineer and engineer processes," he says.

Harding cites a classic example in Netflix, which initially brought content into the home via an envelope in the mailbox that robbed people of the peaceful drive to the video store (remember Blockbuster?), and Uber, that just said, 'what if we got in the car with strangers versus not?'

"From these really simple questions of reimagining the buyer and customer journey they then said, 'well what kind of data would people need to get in a car with a stranger versus not?' What kind of optics, visibility, and predictability could we combine with iPhones and apps and five-star ratings as they reimagined their customer experience using technology? The technology did not create this thinking."

So, marketing and sales functions in the post-sale phases of the journey are now using technology and sharing of data to deliver what Harding calls "delightful, proactive, just-in-time experiences" for customers, which reshapes what the process across the journey looks like.

"It's interesting to see how stark the difference is when we see our marketing, sales, and services organizations who are digitally transforming which look to be fundamentally different levels in their operations enablement frontline leader programs," he says. "The difference can be quite stark depending on the industry and age of the company and kind of how they view their go-to-market functions, whether they're working on it as one unit or whether they're passing things off to each other like an assembly line."

Beyond how the teams manage boundaries in working together in creating compelling experiences for buyers, the other sea change impacting cross-functional team performance in support of customers is managing increasingly through leading indicators versus lagging indicators. But this isn't a trivial activity.

"Even going through an internal process of trying to identify what are the right leading indicators to be monitoring can be tricky," Harding says. "It's not just a no-brainer. You've got to take some thoughtful time to really identify what are the right and appropriate leading indicators that can get you more proactive as opposed to the retrospective. They're not stationary targets."

Making data more visible across teams is especially critical with the emergence of Software as a Service (SaaS) subscription models.

"The SaaS business is like new water on top of an iceberg, your revenue is sitting under the waterline and that's where your competitors come from. What we're seeing is people really need to see data and understand their engagement from the first click on a website to the third step in your implementation process and everyone from marketing, sales and services need to have shared signals."

Figure 4.1 Iceberg

One of the big dangers in trying to create these signals and being laser-focused on gathering large volumes of data is overwhelming staff with the human tendency to rationalize and minimize signals that don't line up with their expected reality.

This was the case for Harding and an operator friend at a leadership meeting in Europe, presenting new sets of data that everyone had to have. And then the special moment came, like at the gym after following a routine of workouts and stepping on a scale and getting a number other than what you expected.

"Our first reaction as humans was this data can't be right like is the scale working right? Let's buy a new tool," he recalls. "It was watching how overwhelmed incredibly smart people were trying to consume what we were looking at. It actually outstripped our collective ability to pass down insights to take actions."

Getting to a place of greater accountability and actionability with people closest to the execution frontlines is key to Harding.

"I have an issue with people who claim to be data-driven. If you're feeling overwhelmed, you don't trust your data, you claim you're data-driven, maybe you're asking too much from the data," he says. "What we really need to do is be very declarative about our strategy, take the time to study what we know about the leading indicators of success, then where we can leverage technology not just to report on those indicators but send signals to the teams. Let's just get it right into the hands of the people who can take action."

So how to counter the unintended impact of setting goals that can overwhelm teams and create bewildered inertia versus focused action? Sometimes it comes down to the old adage of taking things "one step at a time."

I was recently reminded in my personal life of the power of setting clear goals with repetitive tracking and its' relationship to taking meaningful action and achieving real results.

It all started with being invited by a friend and veteran to participate in the 22-day Push-Up Challenge to shine more attention on the very real problem of veteran suicide, sparked by a Veterans Administration report published in 2013 that estimated on average 22 veterans of our armed forces were committing suicide each day. It spoke to my heart and over three weeks, I vigorously pursued my daily goal of recording and posting my 22 pushups on social media (and challenging others in my network to join in).

Then an amazing thing happened. I didn't stop. I incorporated 22 push-ups into my morning routine, regardless of my planned workout that day. Repetition was the key to building both my confidence and upper body strength, which inspired me to set an even more aspirational personal goal of doing a maximum number of reps in 60 seconds as a fundraiser for this very worthy cause.

With the support and planning of an amazing personal trainer, Kristina Teasley of Supreme Strength, I embarked on nearly a ten-month fitness preparation journey that was all about setting continuous volume improvement goals that we not necessarily huge in each increment, but just like the concept of compounding interest, generated amazing results over time. The Friday of each week included three push-up rounds that increased over 40 weeks from 20 seconds each to ultimately 60 seconds each. Only one second was added for each round every week. In the beginning, it seemed like nothing. But over time, it became everything.

By the time challenge day came, I had performed nearly 17,000 pushups! Those 60 seconds went by fast (completing nearly 100) and the consistent, steady build of endurance over those many months made me physically, and mentally, ready to blow through the goal.

Figure 4.2 The Power of Small Increment Goals

The same holds in business. Aggressively setting massively Big, Hairy, and Audacious Goals (BHAGs)

might seem highly motivating but it can also intimidate and be deflating when the tracked results fall well short of those overly big targets. Instead, think about the increased confidence and inspiration that comes from a smaller set of incremental goals, a "rolling thunder" of accomplishment that eventually will excite teams to reflect and say, "how did we come so far before we even knew it?"

According to author and brand researcher **Darshan Mehta**. who for nearly 25 years has been helping companies gain quality brand marketing insights as the founder of iResearch.com, part of that rolling thunder needs to be investing in building your brand. And it all starts with understanding what influences customer behavior.

"If you really think about it, it's really structured curiosity and it's about digging deeper, having a deeper understanding of what really drives people to do something or not do something," he explains. "That's where insights come in and I think oftentimes people misuse the term insights but it's something that can be very valuable to do differentiation, innovation, and also to ultimately to lead to loyalty. It's actually getting to a core truth. I think most people stop at insights as being facts or observations. But it's much more than that."

To better explain the difference between plain data and meaningful insight, Mehta uses the example of a really good comedian that can take things from different parts of society or observations and articulate them into a thought that makes you say, 'Oh my god, that's so true.'

"That's what you're trying to do when you do research, you want to dig deeper to try to get at the core truth that gives you a better understanding of what's really driving a decision."

So, if the quest is for true insights that reflect the drivers of customer behavior companies are trying to influence, one of the biggest pitfalls is becoming too dependent on high volumes of data collection and key performance indicators (KPIs) without fully understanding the "why."

"Especially now with digital, you can get so much information on when people are clicking. You can do a variety of different a/b testing and so on. But it only tells you what people have done," Mehta says. "I'm not saying don't do the KPIs I'm just saying don't overly on them exclusively and that's why I think a lot of mistakes are made and opportunities are forgone because they don't look at the why. And sometimes the competitor really understands the why better."

Mehta cites consumer giant Gillette as a compelling case study. For years their innovation in razors was around going from one blade to two blades to ultimately 5 blades. But that also increased the cost of their razors. And it also altered the customer buying experience because more often the higher-priced razor packages were locked behind glass cabinets at retail, requiring a store employee to open them. As this was all happening, new startups (Dollar Shave Club, Harry's) entered the market offering a convenient, shop-from-home subscription service for razors and fundamentally changed the whole buying experience by taking away market share from an entrenched leader that had at one point owned more than

75% of the traditional market. It's now fallen to roughly 50%.

Whether B2C as in the Gillette example or for hotly contested B2B technology solutions, looking at not just product features but the total customer experience is essential in defining the right actionable insights.

"People are buying more than just products, they're actually buying experiences because on many levels, many products are at a high quality or very equal in terms of their features and benefits," Mehta cautions. "But there is a huge difference in terms of the experience one can have with one product versus another and people now are having to think more and more about looking at the total buying experience from the time they think of it to the interaction with the brand to the actual purchase and even post-purchase."

The act of making a buying decision is both physical and mental.

Sandeep Dayal, a seasoned consultant to global Fortune 500 companies at McKinsey and now Managing Director/ Executive Vice President for Cerenti Marketing Group, has seen firsthand that emotions, not just the sharing of data or factual product information, have a huge impact on customer buying behavior. Extensive research has shown that effectively creating that emotional connection can be very difficult.

"If you are just emotion without it really fitting the moment then it just comes across as unauthentic," he says. "So, there were all these ads that people started doing which would make us laugh, they would make us cry. And what started happening was as people studied those things in neuroscience much more carefully, they found that actually emotions when they are overdone, can be detracting from the message of the brand."

A prime example cited by Dayal is the Apple campaign supported by CEO Steve Jobs that featured a "nerdy PC guy" and the "cool Apple guy." Jobs went out of his way to tell his agency he did not want the ads to be "laugh out loud" funny because his potential customers would focus on the joke and not the product. Research on emotions backs up Jobs' instincts, especially with negative emotions, and when audiences focus on just the emotional story, they forget to focus on the product which is not a good recipe for any marketer.

Figure 4.3 Apple vs. PC Guy Ads

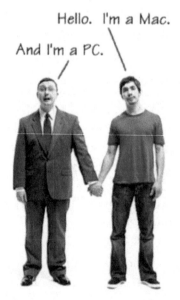

Consuming the information companies provide via their external marketing is indeed a deeply personal experience, with a deeply personal interpretation. Understanding the context of what your audience may be experiencing, or feeling when you reach them is also very critical.

Take Facebook. Launching a Super Bowl Ad featuring the Metaverse (a play on their company re-branded as Meta), the attempt to be funny by depicting animated band members being displaced from playing at a restaurant closing down than showing a particular band member being humiliated in a series of scenes before being reunited with the band hit too close to home for many who have lost their jobs and income from the pandemic.

"You have to be very careful when you play with people's emotions. When you show a particular ad with a particular intent, they will interpret it with their intent. Not your intent," Dayal says.

"Good marketing revolves around getting inside people's heads and really understanding what is that connection that you can make with customers," he adds. "So far that has been very difficult to do because what goes on in a person's head is very personal and it's very difficult to dive into those things. You can look at fields like cognitive psychology, behavioral economics, social anthropology, and even linguistics. The one common thing is they've been trying to understand human behavior and how the human mind works and as a result over the last fifteen to twenty years we have a lot better understanding."

The revelation according to Dayal is that the mind attaches sort of an "aura" around things. Everything we see about a person or hear from their speech is not everything there is to them. Understanding people is about getting into their souls and their personalities.

The same holds for brands and when our brains see a particular product.

"So, there is the seen and the unseen and it is that unseen which is so important toward what a brand can be," he points out. "The beauty of the unseen is that it can get you that true and lasting differentiation that you're looking for in your brand which you cannot get if the only thing that you do is product differentiation."

Gathering meaningful data through ongoing brand research is a wise investment. There are quantitative approaches, with the advanced automation capabilities of artificial intelligence and machine learning with big data, which can overshadow more traditional qualitative approaches. But according to Dayal, maintaining a balanced mix of research methods is essential.

"I always advocate to my clients to be really good at your qualitative research and do it in many different ways, do focus groups, do metaphor elicitation do ethnographic studies. Get in front of your consumers and really talk to them so you can gain some insights on that which you will never get by just letting machines do it."

Tim Parkin is a global marketing advisor and coach to market leaders for some of the world's most renowned brands, helping their teams contribute even better to accelerated growth. He agrees that customer focus and consistently gathering customer data is key, but points out that there can be a measurable difference between what customers *say* and what they *do*.

"If you want to focus on the customer you have to understand how they think and how they act and if you want to improve conversations or optimize your marketing," he says. "This is essential and part of this is talking to customers, surveying them, customer interviews, that sort of thing. That is only a piece of the equation because you can't trust what people tell you and I mean that you know politely and generously. What people say is not necessarily how they act so you have to watch what I do, not what I say and that is what we mean by behavioral thinking and behavioral psychology."

Sometimes it is about using data to make subtle shifts in marketing execution.

Parkin shares a compelling example of a client campaign that increased conversion by 329% by making a simple change in the page flow of a prospect's journey on their website. At first, the client had their prospects start with learning about the application program they were selling on their website, then hope they would choose to move to a separate page to apply for it. Asking people why they did not apply produced answers like high pricing among other things. But when Parkin's team looked closer at the data on how people used the site and walked through different pages, they realized prospects were not fully sold yet and they had outstanding questions about the program and how it would benefit them. Knowing this was a catalyst for meaningful action.

"Based on this analysis, we decided to add a page before all this, telling them about the industry and it would paint this vision for them of who they could become and what this would mean for them and this is completely counterintuitive by the way. No one in marketing wants to make the process longer. By doing this it presold them on this future vision, and this was not about answering their questions or anything like that. This is emotional. This is the psychology part of it and their behavior and so by the time they got to the program page it was just about the logistics. And so we saw this huge massive jump in conversion."

The significant impact of data extends well beyond customers and prospects. It is a cornerstone to better understanding your competitive position in the market.

Lori Cooper Wolfe, Head of Business Insights and Analytics at OSG, has spent her entire career perfecting the art of effective competitive analytics and intelligence. Unlike traditional market research which may be providing both an inside and an outside lens, she defines competitive intelligence as being focused on having "one foot outside the company" in spending as much as 75% of the time looking externally and then bringing it back with the remaining 25% of existing company knowledge to help leaders be more proactive than reactive.

Getting this process right does not happen instantly, requiring some deep reflection and brutal honesty.

"It takes time. It's not something that is going to happen right away. And when you start to get into predictive analytics, you need to be able to look backward to see patterns over time," she cautions. "The company who really does well with a competitive or market intelligence function is one that isn't really afraid to say the emperor is not wearing any clothes a lot of time."

Setting deeply rooted biases in assessing the competitive landscape can be hard, and often hiring from outside into newly created roles works best so you have the people driving this activity day-to-day coming at it from a truly fresh, unbiased perspective. Cooper Wolfe notes that as more companies invest in gathering competitive and market data, the lines between roles in Market Research, Analytics, and Intelligence are blurring a bit into a new, powerful word called *insights*.

But at the end of the day, successful outcomes from the data gathering and interpretation will be driven by having clarity of purpose up front.

"The thing you really need to do is figure out what questions you are trying to answer," she says. Popular tools in formulating strategy, like SWOT analyses or competitor profiles, become less relevant without having clear, relevant goals.

"What is it doing for you if your fundamental question is how your strategy differs from competitors and is that something we should be concerned about? So, there are some people you deal with who never really get to asking the right questions, but there will be other people you can teach about asking questions and there probably are some high-level strategy people who've got burning issues they have to resolve."

Using data to increase intelligence around audience engagement or your competitors is one thing. How to manage huge volumes of data securely is quite another. In a time of countless breaches and exposure, having sound data security strategies and policies in the collection, storage and analysis is essential to minimize risk to the more valuable corporate assets. Nowhere is this truer than with the exploding volume of video communications.

Clive Sawkins is COO of the Tech Collaboration Division of New Era Technology and former CEO of Pinnaca. In leading a high-growth global company helping demanding customers rapidly scale their video collaboration capabilities, he is acutely aware of how important maintaining security is.

"We came at this at another direction very early on which is if we're going to offer secure communications then we better really mean it and security comes at multiple levels. It's not just turning on firewalls, if it was that easy then everyone would be doing it," he says.

"But how are you going to secure content? How are your processes going to manage things like GDPR and customer data management? How are you going to integrate that into a workflow and an architecture? How are you going to encrypt calls?

Peeling back the onion of encryption reveals the need for a very unique strategy, for every call or each leg of the call, that encompasses the very essence of an organization.

"Security comes at a multiple set of levels and you have

to build it into your culture," Sawkins advises. "You have to build it into your network design. You have to build it into your applications and then when you think you've done it, you start again. This is a process that is never going to stop around security now, and it has to be totally ingrained in everything that you do. When we get back to the new normal a lot of organizations are going to have to reassess what they did and work out what actually does that fit within a security architecture and did they put any of their customer data at a liability in that environment. I think the pendulum has swung very quickly to the right, and now it's going to have to swing back to the middle a little bit again."

When it comes to data, Sawkins is passionate about secure management being a market focus for the foreseeable future.

"People will start to take this seriously again. No one needs me to point out how many email trojans have been put out there, how many emails are spamming and taking an opportunity at the moment to confuse people. You've got to protect yourself and your businesses from all of that every day of the week," he advises.

The overwhelming growth of data sources and data volume can itself create barriers in organizations to best prepare for security threats to their most valuable assets.

Steve Prentice knows this all too well. An expert in organizational psychology who has helped countless global technology companies focus on the junction where people and technology interact and who specializes in human acceptance of cyber security, artificial intelligence, and blockchain, he sees the exponential growth of data volume validating fundamental laws of human behavior.

"It's kind of like a mixture of Moore's law and Parkinson's law," he suggests. "Moore's law stated the more storage space you have the more you'll need because we just keep putting more data in there. Parkinson's law states that work expands to fill the time available. In this case, you know data expands to fill the need available. It becomes kind of like a panacea that we feel if we have more data then we have more control over our circumstances. But there comes a point where too much data becomes pure overload just in the time and resources required to process it."

So, what to do as a leader in better managing your data to ensure it is a truly productive and safe asset? Develop your human capacities through training and continuous learning.

"Digital literacy is the capacity to be able to understand data and work with it on both a corporate level but also on an individual level. How to, for instance, determine whether an email coming into your inbox is legitimate or if it is a spam scam email. Digital literacy is that human capacity to evolve into the place we are now at technologically to be able to handle the data that requires, once again, a greater focus on training and learning on all levels to recognize that," Prentice notes. "It's the same thing if you wanted to learn how to swim and somebody takes you out into the middle of the Pacific Ocean and say 'okay, try.' It's kind of really the worst place to try and learn how to swim. But that's where we're at in terms of managing data and assuming that if we manage the data our problems would be solved and that is not the case."

For **Sushila Nair**, VVice President, Security Services for global IT infrastructure and services provider NTT Data Services, the sudden onset of the global pandemic in 2020 brought on additional challenges in crafting effective data security strategies.

"The current situation has really accelerated digital transformation. Maybe they were using a little bit of the cloud, now they're using a whole lot of the cloud," she says. "Before maybe they had supported 10% to 20% of their workforce working from home, now they support 100% or 90%, so all of those changes introduce risk."

While acknowledging the many heroic examples of transforming major company support processes, like call centers, and entire offices to a remote model—sometimes in less than one week—Nair cautions that some of this transformation likely came without sound security strategies. The surge in virtual communications and collaboration has created even more questions.

"Have they really gone through and secured that now that we're collaborating? We're working with business partners, maybe clients all on the same system. Wonderful, where we want to be, but how do you know you're not sharing information that has privacy implications or security implications or ipr implications?" she asks. "The real challenge there for most organizations is to understand where they are today and understanding that their threat landscape has changed."

Nair calls out an additional human factor beyond just

recognizing threats and understanding implications.

"For many organizations, they have the additional challenge of not having the right skills and enough people because they have to move now very quickly to actually bolster up their security," she says. "Because they've had so much rapid change, many of their people may not have all the right skills. You know they're more familiar with on-premise, maybe more traditional forms of security, not perhaps cloud-based security which is where they need to go so, we've got gaps in knowledge. We've got increased risk."

Combined with increased costs of effectively supporting all this rapid change, a financial reality that Nair refers to as "COVID economics", leaders have no choice but to prioritize developing a well-aligned, clear strategy for securing their assets, including critical data. Technology that enables even greater capture of mission-critical data is a huge opportunity for companies to break away from the competition but must be done collaboratively and wisely.

"Organizations that come out of the pandemic stronger than others are the organizations that really kind of subscribed to this idea of this adaptive workforce, this moving away from silos and really embedding security in everything that we do," she points out. "Application development has moved toward being faster and more agile and pushing out new features more quickly and how did they do that without losing security was to build security experts into these scrum teams. This isn't some kind of a doctor's checkup at the end of a business process where we go, ok, security person come in now and tell us how we did. We have to imbed it all the way through."

"The technology of today is allowing you to reinvent yourself. It is only limited by your imagination, and we can do incredible things. By doing that, also understand when you use technology to reinvent yourself, it because your greatest strength and it can also become your greatest weakness because it will be a point of attack. You also have to secure yourself."

As Marketing strategies and tactics continue to be reshaped via automation technology, they will continue to be significantly reliant on disciplined and focused data collection for success.

Dan McGaw, a self-described "data nerd" and Founder/ CEO of Mcgaw.io, a fast-growing revenue infrastructure and analytics agency, sees data as the foundational core of the current era of technology-driven marketing. And he sees a major void between formal marketing education and the skills needed to be successful in modern marketing.

"Marketing technology is getting to a super technical place. There's not a good educational system to teach people the fundamentals of marketing tech. Some of the most important technology processes that we're just not made aware of that are the most foundational part of marketing tech is how do you build out your taxonomy for your data," he says. "Taxonomy is the data dictionary of how your tools will talk and share data together. This is a foreign concept to most marketers."

McGaw does recognize there has been a bit of an increase in available courses and new communities teaching traditional marketers more scientific marketing skills, but still a real gap that makes the full transition a big lift.

An entrepreneur since age 13 and not a classic marketer by education, McGaw has benefited from amazing marketing mentors and argues that successful marketing today blends art with science.

"My team is more science-based. To be successful in the modern marketing world, especially after COVID, you've got to get more science-based. If you can't understand how the science actually works, it makes it really hard to come up with marketing campaigns, and to lead a team to do an effective marketing campaign because it is extremely science-based now."

As a very busy advisor and consultant, McGaw has seen the extremes of very good—and very bad—data management. His observation is the smartest approach to getting the most from marketing data boils down to a couple of key things.

First, they have a good taxonomy and data dictionary. Second, they utilize some type of a customer data platform (CDP) to track customer touchpoints in building a more accurate "360" view, funneling marketing data into a behavioral analytics tool. Third, they use Google Analytics and also using data from CDP to funnel their data into their Customer Relationship Management (CRM) and Marketing Automation tools.

"They're trying to recycle all of their data about their

customers to all the tools they can," McGaw says. "If a sales rep updates Salesforce, that information goes to Marketing Automation, but it also goes into a behavioral analytics tool. The really, really sophisticated companies that are winning the game are the ones using some sort of export tool to pull the data from all these platforms and then dump it into a warehouse."

By then sticking analytics products like Tableau or Looker on top of it, and leveraging business intelligence tools, McGaw finds these forward-thinking companies who have built their own warehouse can develop custom data models and report on all kinds of numbers to better drive their business.

The next level in data management evolution, such as McGaw's client Service Titan (valued at over $8 billion) is all about getting clean data in, then using data science, machine learning, and AI to predict what is going to be good outcomes, or potential bad outcomes to know better where to focus their business.

"It's a high-class thing to get to," he says. "It's out of the reach for some companies just due to the talent they require or the budget they have, but it is a priority you need to make."

Speaking of budget, a very fundamental and traditional part of most marketing budgets is event marketing, the engagement with prospects and customers in virtual or live events (conferences, trade shows, webinars, and the like).

A common question asked by CMOs to their event

managers is "What kind of return on investment am I getting from these major event investments?" Advances in event data collection technology are playing a big role in creating higher quality responses but challenges remain.

Peter Gillett, CEO of Zuant, has developed event solutions enabling far more intelligent lead capture utilizing mobile devices. Transforming to a purely virtual event world during a pandemic onset and then back again to a hybrid event environment has been a jarring ride for many event strategists, yet an environment of high change doesn't diminish the critical role data analytics in better decision making. With so many different applications on the market, the potential for creating non-integrated silos in data collection and management is high.

"There's still a problem with making data and analytics interesting to people because it's not a classical creative marketing to the design area," he says.

Gillett notes that 10-20 years ago, the landscape was dominated by big platforms that presumably allowed for compression of all data in a single place, with each aspect of those systems updated and data updated. Today we live in a much more decentralized world of disparate systems that are crying out for technology providers to step up with new systems integration solutions.

"Now we've gone the other way and each of these specialist software applications, they're all brilliant in what they do whether it's marketing information, or call center systems, events technologies, and so on. But the problem is that the ownership of those systems has now been distributed out to special users of course and for some reason, the integration aspects don't get full of very much, and therefore you've got customer data, prospect data at different stages of evolution within the same organization, within the same specialty application."

"I think the focus of our industries is to be able to have a central, single version of the proof which updates every other system because unless we cross that bridge and get that in place, we can't really do all that really nice analytics and it becomes difficult to do market penetration studies or salespeople to follow up on leads if their own data hasn't been updated in light of customer calls that have come into a call center."

Brianna Haag is the Director of Demand Generation for Hopin, a rapidly growing event analytics solution provider that works with event managers around the world in creating high-ROI event experiences. The recent explosive growth of online events has created new access to more real-time data that can make a huge difference in tying in related content to post-event follow-ups and relationship development with prospects.

"We encourage teams to take advantage of the really good content that we can follow up with in addition to the recording if there's a white paper or a blog post or something that's related to what the event was about and the topic at hand," she says. "Something that I think is so cool about the information and data that's available to you now as an event organizer that does an online experience is you can really get personal with your follow-up. So, if someone spends a lot of time in the expo hall at a couple of booths or you know they attended one session instead of another or you see that there were really interested and engaged in the chat during a particular session."

The greater personalization that comes with fully virtual or even hybrid events is enabling a more specific application of behavioral analytics.

"Hosting an in-person event, you don't know someone's movement. You don't know which content was landing for them. You have all that data now with an online experience. You know your prospects or customer or people part of your community and your audience in a way that makes most sense for them. That's where you can really make even more of an impact because it's more relevant, it's more strategic to inform the way we communicate."

Increasing your visibility and using the latest technology tools to track data doesn't of course create transformative outcomes in and of itself. The power of data lies in both the *quality* of data that is gathered plus the *interpretation* that drives decisions and action.

The financial cost of relying on bad data, or misinterpreting data, is shockingly high. Gartner Research estimates the average financial impact of poor data quality on organizations is $9.7 million annually. An IBM study discovered in the U.S. alone, businesses lose $3.1 trillion (!) annually due to poor data quality.

Figure 4.4 Data Usage

Peter Shafer, Vice President of Sales and Marketing at Everest Communications, a digital communications firm providing counsel and execution support in the areas of analytics, social media strategy, and digital reputation repair, has research in his veins. Starting his career at leading polling firms Gallup and Harris, he has seen many companies stall out in their struggle to deeply and accurately interpret collected data in the quest for better decision-making. But following a few simple principles can make a huge difference.

"Number one, you need to recognize data is an asset, it's not just a static piece of information. There is value to it and if you look at it as an asset, you're going to acknowledge that there is an importance to it, that there is value to it, and that you are able to use it in a productive way," says Shafer.

The next step is making sure you clearly define what types of data you need to achieve the insights you're looking for. Sounds simple. Not so fast....

"That's where the one stumbling block is hit, is that organizations and leaders don't have the right data to

121

make the decision and then they use convenient sources of data to make the decision. Oftentimes, just asking the right question is more important than trying to create that perfect question."

Shafer sees a final best practice as having a clear set of desired outcomes. An effective approach he took at Gallup and Harris required adopting the mindset of a journalist.

"One of the things we would ask clients to do before collecting data was to write a draft headline of what they would like the story to look like or what they would like the data to say so we had an idea of how to structure the questions," he recalls.

This allowed for better identifying who to talk to, what to be looking for when the data came back, and avoiding falling into the trap of just trying to gather as much data as possible and hoping for clarity.

"It was also a good exercise in kind of being a devil's advocate to the client to say 'is this really what you want? Is this really going to be that important to you and then finally are you going to be able to actually make a decision off of that'?"

Shafer admits it is a humbling thing to set ego aside and admit a ready answer to senior executive questions is not currently in hand. The pressure of an organization needing measurable performance improvement can lead to very short-term decisions. The key is to think in periods of time versus points in time, to avoid the cultural and financial consequences or rushing bad decisions.

TAKEAWAYS CHECKLIST:

☑ Generating demand is art and science, becoming most effective when informed by data that includes leading indicators to future performance

☑ The "push-up principle" proves the power of consistency and repetition in measuring your results, leading to exponential improvement

☑ Personalization, application of behavioral analytics, and being realistic in assessing data quality are crucial for maximizing the effectiveness of your data in driving better decision making

5

Exceptional Leadership

---

lead·er·ship – *the action of leading a group of people or an organization*

Regardless of the products or services it offers, an organization's greatest asset is its people.

Peter Drucker made the now-famous observation that *"culture eats strategy for breakfast."* This does not mean that strategy is not important, it simply calls out the fact that culture is ultimately a more powerful determinant of long-term success. And what defines any culture are human attitudes, behaviors, communications, priorities, and values that are both nourished—and nurtured—by leaders.

The classic definition of leadership is framed by hierarchy, through organizational charts with a more select few at the top responsible for the masses below. The truth is, while the *action* of leadership does and needs to occur from people with the title and responsibility for managing others, its application does not *require* formal authority over, or responsibility for, others. The most vibrant and impactful company cultures evolve when everyone—regardless of role or status level—provides inspiration and motivation in support of a common mission.

But people leaders have a unique opportunity every day to be a catalyst for great outcomes from their teams. A fundamental question I have constantly asked myself throughout my career in leading global teams small and large, representing a full spectrum of diversity of age, gender, race, and language, is what separates truly *exceptional* leadership from merely good enough?

What has evolved is a personal philosophy built first and foremost on respecting people, enabling them to continuously grow and maximize the full potential of their contributions. This has happened alongside the strengthening of my own "Servant Leader" mindset, placing the interests and needs of my team members above my self-interests and needs. The focus of this leadership approach is on personal development, authentic actions, building a sense of community, and sharing power. It has been an amazing journey in seeing elevated team performance and numerous team members grow professionally into executive roles, "paying it forward" through the leadership of their own teams.

I call the foundation of my philosophy the Leadership Triad, three guiding principles with supporting questions that have proven invaluable in maximizing team performance and team morale.

Figure 5.1 Triad

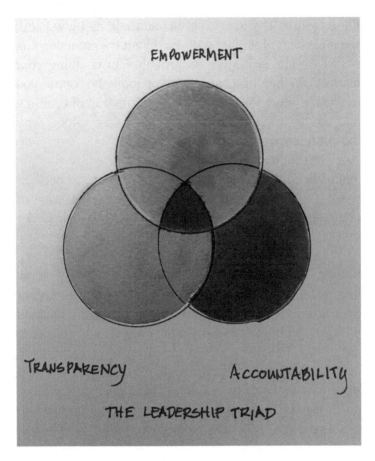

EMPOWERMENT

TRANSPARENCY

ACCOUNTABILITY

THE LEADERSHIP TRIAD

The first principle is Empowerment. *How can I empower my team while continuing to prioritize a servant-leader mindset?*

People feel the most respected and do their best work when fully empowered. We've all known the "hovering" manager at some point in our careers, the person that goes deep into the weeds and micromanages their teams to death. By their actions what they are telling their team is "I don't trust you to do the job I've asked you to do to the standards I've set." Without sunlight and good soil, the most beautiful plant will die. Placing a proactive box over the plant will stunt its growth. But enabling your teams to do their best work is never about the control you exert. The more you focus on control instead of enabling and empowering, your impact diminishes (along with the confidence of your team).

Teams need the challenge, and the freedom, to do their work—with enthusiastic coaching along the way of course—but with the implicit message from their leader that "I know you can do this!"

Rather than chasing a superiority complex, show vulnerability and humility by sharing examples of your own mistakes. Navigate through the inevitable ups and with your teams by monitoring the pressure and providing outlets for releasing pressure rather than fixating on accelerating pressure to the breaking point because you were told that is what leaders who demand excellence do. You will build mutual respect and commitment to places you never thought possible!

We have all seen the "smartest person in the room" syndrome when leaders make it their mission to remind everyone, that *they* have all the answers, are the ultimate "source of truth," are uniquely qualified to make key decisions, and most importantly, dispense continuous critiques as a reminder of these "facts." I had a senior leader in my organization several years ago who habitually had his leadership team report for "whiteboard" reflective sessions that frankly were an exercise in them espousing their version of "truth" (meaning the failing of others) and everyone else dutifully listening. What a deflating, un-empowering experience, where power, status, and control trumped authentic collaboration. Once you condition your team for this repeated kind of experience, their inner fire snuffs out over time and they become increasingly disinterested, disappointed, and reactionary.

Don't get me wrong, constructive reflection is a real opportunity for all of us. But when critiques and constructive feedback are done in a vacuum, without the authenticity of conveying a personal belief in the full potential of each of your team members, what your team hears you saying more than anything else is "I don't know why there is no one that is getting the job done like I am."

The second principle is Transparency. *Am I transparent in all communications, the good news, and the not-so-good news?*

All companies are populated by human beings who thrive off communication and connectedness. When leaders become highly selective about who they share with and what they share, trust goes out the window. Basics like informational updates cascaded from senior leadership are okay, what is even better in building a strong connection to your teams is a regular cadence of a visual team or one-ones (in-person or by video conference).

Research shows that body language is vital when it comes to communication. Not just how you say something, but your facial expressions and body posture matter—all of the things that get lost in emails. A UCLA study found around 93% of communication effectiveness is determined by nonverbal cues. Integrity is defined by being honest with your team members about where things stand with your company, including financial performance, organizational structures, people departures, and more. No leader *wants* to deliver bad news, it means you're human if it makes you feel uncomfortable.

Exceptional leaders make sure to never put their selfish comforts first by taking an easy or lazy way of avoiding directly communicating tough news, which sometimes steals dignity from their team members. Unfortunately, I've seen this play out many times with organizational restructures, where sudden, unexpected same-day departures by highly experienced, strong performers are designed to minimize any real interactions other than an explanatory post-departure email.

Servant leadership is about personal sacrifice. This hit home in a very personal way several years back when my role was eliminated as part of a company downsizing. My manager delivered the news unexpectedly in a one-on-one, which included the timing of "effective immediately" with the heads up my team had been gathered together in a conference room to hear the news…from him, with the expectation I would "prefer" to quietly gather my things and exit the building! Stunned silence, fear, all the emotions that come in a moment like that. But as I heard the words finally coming from my mouth that no, I was going to walk over to that conference room to share the news and say goodbye the way the team deserved, an amazing thing happened. Even though I was the one who was getting the ax in that office, I felt elevated…and he seemed a bit more diminished. Through sheer force of will, I sat in front of my entire team managing a sea of emotions to let them know how much the privilege of working with them, experiencing our successes, and getting through the challenges, meant to me. It was emotional. My voice cracked, and there were some tears. It was damn hard. But my team let me know at the moment, and in some correspondence after the fact, how much they appreciated and respected my courage in doing it.

Figure 5.2 We vs. I

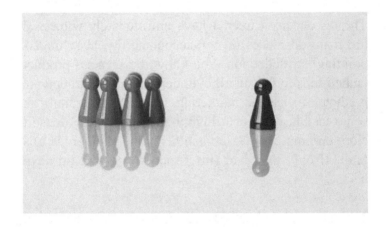

The third principle is Accountability. *Are we mutually accountable for performance and results?*

The late Pat Summitt, coach of the University of Tennessee women's basketball team for 38 years and who retired as the winningest college basketball coach of all time, was a passionate champion for accountability.

"Responsibility equals accountability equals ownership. And a sense of ownership is the most powerful weapon a team or organization can have," Summit observed.

Accountability is about prioritizing delivering on commitments, in essence, to do what you say you will do. It is about integrity, and being honest to acknowledge when things don't turn out as expected. It is about wherever possible measuring what we do. Celebrating key accomplishments, and learning from mistakes in continually getting better. Exceptional leaders walk the talk in practicing personal accountability and in coaching their teams to do the same.

Throughout my career, I have unfortunately witnessed too many instances of non-accountability, aka "finger-pointing" or deflection. You know the scene: a product launch fails to fire on all cylinders and doesn't generate predicted metrics, a marketing campaign falls short on some visible KPIs or a highly anticipated sale doesn't close on time. "It's (insert another name or other team)'s fault. If only they had (insert action), we would have been OK."

Taking an "us-them" mindset is a convenient but destructive escape hatch from self-reflection on what *you as a leader* and what *your team* could have done better to deliver the desired results. Show me a team leader that stands up and says "it's on me" versus finger-pointing deflection and nine times out of ten you'll show me a team that is courageously taking risks and practicing continuous improvement.

A powerful way for leaders to create more visible accountability is the use of dashboards (metrics tracking frameworks) and the repeated use of a post-project reflection process, historically called a "post-mortem" (nobody died!) but more appropriately referred to as a "retrospectives." Best facilitated by a more objective, neutral party (a project manager from a Program Management Office is ideal), the idea is to shift participants' mindsets away from "who is to blame for our failure?" to "what can we learn to do better in the future?" The more visual you can make the retrospective the better, using collaborative tools like a Miro board encourages vivid capture of key learnings, creating a healthy sense of shared accountability by all functions who worked together on a project.

There are other tools, behaviors, and concepts that exceptional leaders employ to boost the performance of their teams.

I have known **Steve Gutzler**, a best-selling author, motivational speaker, business coach, and founder of Leadership Quest, for more than two decades. I have seen firsthand his transformational impact while teaching some of my actual teams to understand that business success over the long term is not a matter of just fine-tuning their technical skills.

"Your IQ, your technical skills, actually get you in the game," he says. "But in how far you advance, emotional intelligence really becomes the number one predictor of success and high performance. It's simply recognizing the impact of the emotions that you bring to the workplace, that mood, that attitude that emotion you bring every single day. How you influence people with those emotions, but helping other people recognize the power of their emotions in the workplace."

According to Gutzler, elevating their leadership game boils down to being honest with themselves about what's most important in developing meaningful connections with their teams.

"Leaders today need to turn up the dimmer switch regarding self-awareness, understanding that emotional impact, understanding your strengths and weaknesses, understanding that social skills are not soft, they're hard-edged leadership skills that really lead to high performance."

Gutzler argues that organizations need to put an equivalent emphasis on personal development and helping their people grow in self-awareness as they do their strategy development, vision, goal building, financial management, or hiring. Ultimately this pays off by reaching full potential by building stronger emotional connections with clients, creating emotional connections with team members, and greater overall employee loyalty. He suggests rather than targeting this development for a select few at the highest levels of your organization, the greatest impact happens when driving greater emotional intelligence across *all* levels.

"Bring everybody. If you can grow leaders at every level, think about that. If you grow the leadership competencies of your organization, it will give you the competitive edge," Gutzler says. "If you can grow leaders at every level, grievances will go down. Greater collaboration will go up. Impact for your organization will go up. Sales will go up. Often, we're trying to sell things and tell clients about our services, but not really listening. The very first step to success is to understand the needs, wants, and desires of your clients and that's all around increasing your emotional intelligence skills."

The financial and performance costs of low emotional intelligence can be staggering. Research shows as many as 80% of people leaving an organization are leaving because of their relationship with a single manager. The resulting costs in turnover, lost productivity, re-tooling and training can really add up. By developing leadership skills that include the ability to establish meaningful connections through emotional intelligence, Gutzler has seen turnover rates decrease by as much as 60%, sales increase by as much as 20%, and the leadership culture grows by 10 to 12%—where the entire organization view of leadership is no longer defined by a positional title. The culture starts believing that everyone can lead. How powerful is that!

Gutzler reminds us that a big part of exceptional leadership is being a positive energy source for their teams. While we can all experience the doldrums, like the great sailing ships of the past hitting patches of no wind—including negative self-talk—exceptional managers realize they can have the most profound impact when they engage their teams with positivity. Self-confident leaders project positivity and tend to be more centered, with a strong sense of values.

"People are attracted to the light. When we display darkness with our vocabulary, it is a dead end," he says. "Our self-talk, our vocabulary, and our actions will either attract or repel people. Shift from victim to leader."

A big part of emotional intelligence is empathy and

situational awareness. Exceptional leaders understand that *context* is everything in making a positive impact versus a detrimental impact in their engagement with others. The time, the place, the method, and most importantly the words chosen in your interactions are of course powerful determinants of *results*.

I was painfully reminded of this many years ago as I was struggling to build a stronger relationship with a new manager who brought a vastly different style than what I had been accustomed to. Where my prior manager was a deep, cerebral, and sensitive soul who promoted dialogue, expression of feelings, and healthy collaboration, my new manager was far more aloof, brash, clinical, and directive.

We had very different styles and over time I knew the state of the relationship, of feeling respected and supported, wasn't where it had been with my previous manager. After several months, when I was invited to join him for a one-on-one breakfast in the restaurant of the venue on the morning of day one of an intense multi-day team offsite, an event I was going to play a key role in as a meeting note taker and facilitator. This was an unusual type of request from him, I assumed this was an effort to clear the air and build some bridges toward a more positive place. Wrong.

Instead, over eggs and toast in a crowded dining room, I was subjected to his sharing his assessment of me as a failure in my position, describing the strong relationship I had formed with field teams as largely meaningless, and questioning my suitability for a more senior leadership role. The challenge wasn't the *idea* of being honest and constructive with a managerial point of view on performance, something I have delivered myself more than a few times during quarterly-, mid-year, or end-of-year reviews. In this very one-way versus interactive conversation, the lack of authenticity, of his not showing a clear *desire* for me to succeed is what stood out the most. Exceptional leaders will accept responsibility and show humility in asking themselves what role they may have in the performance outcomes of each team member. Given the timing and setting, this experience wasn't elevated, it was deflating. It felt mean-spirited and selfish. Needless to say, within a few months I had moved on from that particular leader to a much better situation.

According to **Ben Gibson**, former CMO at Aruba Networks, Veritas, F5 Networks, and Nutanix, exceptional marketing leadership is about creating iconic signature moments that rally customers, partners, and employees around a specific big idea. These big memorable moments can be triggered by a wide variety of things, from high-visibility product launches to sales kickoff events to new brand campaigns, IPO, and many more. And a blueprint for success comes from the world of entertainment.

"As a CMO you have to think like a Hollywood producer or director," he says. "When I was a kid until now, I've always been fascinated by Hollywood. Disney is a great example of this particularly when they bought my favorite Hollywood franchise, Star Wars. Disney was the master of this when they launched the latest Star Wars trilogy, how they ignited their grassroots that could be a user conference for a tech company or a sales kickoff to get the enthusiasts in local markets to really get excited. So being a marketing leader is borrowing and being inspired by the industry, for me it's Hollywood. Choose your entertainment medium and I think there's some great lesson to be learned about how you cut through the noise."

Gibson sees the path to exceptional as also being paved by having high-quality standards for your hires.

"Hire smarter than you are. It's not to make you look better, it's to bring someone in so they can advance, and you never miss an opportunity to shine a bright light on them," he recommends. "Sometimes because you're running fast, you have to check some of your ego at the door when you ascend to a CMO. You don't always have the be the person on the main stage. I've had wonderful people that worked for me where I tried to make sure that they were main stage, that they were presenting in different venues. Sometimes it had to be me, but I tried to find opportunities for that to happen because the best companies in the world do wonderful succession planning.

Figure 5.3 Succession Planning

Ensuring greater visibility for your team members is a key long-term investment.

"As a leader, you're measured by boards that look at this carefully, by 'okay, who do you have on your staff that could be an immediate successor to you if you were God forbid hit by a bus?' You can't have that experience or that capability unless you're hiring smarter than you are," Gibson says. "That could be with a unique experience, it could be some brilliant people in terms of background education that you don't have. You can learn from them. You help them grow and those are the folks that really exceed expectations across the board."

Michelle Accardi, CEO of Logically, one of the fastest Managed Service Providers in the U.S., strongly agrees that enabling her teams to do more and receive greater visibility is the formula for long-term success.

"Going from an operating role of a COO or a CMO to a CEO, one of the biggest challenges for me was to let go of all the doing myself and learn to empower other people to shine their light and deliver the value of the company and to themselves," she reflects.

"That's one of the biggest hurdles I think for a lot of leaders who are successful because we tend to be great executors and have a great strategy, but for me specifically the tough part has been enabling everyone else, empowering everyone else to be the ones who get to do the work. As I've moved up in roles it's become more apparent how important it is to have a full team of people who are executing. Without it, you simply can't reach scale.

Accardi has also seen how critical empathy has been for her to deliver exceptional leadership, a caring for her team on a very human level which has meant being there for support when life throws its' curveballs.

Case in point: an employee in her former company that came to Accardi for a very personal conversation about the fact her three stepchildren had recently lost their mother and now she and her husband knew they had to step into some bigger shoes to take care of all of them—plus another half-brother. That employee had witnessed Accardi's commitment to striking a balancing act between a strong technology leader and nurturing mother. So, she asked her if she would be willing to adopt her 17-year-old stepdaughter's twins! This ask was driven by the employee observing how Accardi approached her team communications and support.

"She said when she had questions I didn't just sit at my desk, I got up and I walked her to the person I felt could give her their best answer, and I stayed until I knew I understood," Accardi says. "That's what she wanted for her grandchildren, she wanted them to have someone who's going to be invested in them."

Accardi keeps a high sense of connection with all of her employees at Logically by holding a thirty-minute collaboration call every week. This is not a timeslot for senior leadership to do all the talking, it is intended as an open forum to discuss weekly happenings and for employees to share with her their major challenges.

"It takes a level of collaboration to make that work across and create scale for the organization and for our customers, enabling people to sort of talk openly, ask questions and I think it's really helping to set culture," she observes.

Fostering an environment that motivates employees to reach their full potential is as important in large, resource-rich organizations as it is in start-ups or small businesses.

Steve Reasner is the Chief Innovation Officer for LIFTInnovate, a consulting firm focused on technology adoption, outcome-based consulting, and the incubation of innovative solutions that strategically leverage innovation to create transformative results. Exceptional leaders understand what he calls "people-powered growth." And at the heart of it all is enablement.

"What fuels an organization is the people and how do we enable them to be successful? If we're growing our people and really focused, that's what's going to drive growth," he says. "It's going to keep them engaged and want to do more. People-powered growth is how do we enable them for success. How do we give them tools and processes and how do we listen and how do we continue to grow over time."

Exceptional leadership is also about the ability to understand and embrace shifts in your macro environment that necessitate changing direction, changing priorities, and an entirely new mindset. Sometimes this change in direction is necessary as part of a new vision or evolving strategy.

For **Lisa Jasper**, Founder and CEO of Thought Ensemble and Managing VP at Pariveda, who consults with companies on intentional business transformation, it is all about being able to pivot with a purpose. Not change for change's sake, but adaptive leadership and personal growth that can help lift organizations to higher performance. And as disruptive and stressful as the onset of a global pandemic was, it was also a catalyst for her to evolve into an even more impactful leader.

"I've grown a lot. I think the timing for me was really fortuitous as a leader, I had stepped in as CEO just a couple of years ago and I was just really getting comfortable and enjoying my role when the pandemic happened, and also, I had gone through a leadership assessment," she says. "The development areas that came up through that were exactly what I needed to navigate our company through this. Our team loved that I was inclusive, but they also wanted me to be a little more vocal about my opinion on things if we were needing to move really quickly and make quick decisions. It gave me permission and confidence to step into my role when we needed it most."

In baseball, effective hitting is about making specific, sometimes subtle adjustments at the plate to different pitch styles. In Jasper's case, this was about strengthening her confidence and tenacity to navigate through challenging times.

"I'm probably just a lot more comfortable stepping up as a leader and I'm definitely more resilient to curve balls. I think every time we go through hard times, we're more resilient."

We all face curve balls in our work life and our personal life. Some small, some beyond our comprehension that test our courage, our strength, and even our will to live. Exceptional leaders figure out how to produce meaningful learning moments from even the most challenging of circumstances.

Author, technology executive, and co-founder of WeWomenLead **Alison Conigliaro-Hubbard** knows how to navigate big challenges in complex, dynamic global organizations from her time at Cisco and Riverbed Technology. But she faced her biggest challenge ever on a much more personal level when she unexpectedly received a diagnosis of Stage 3 endometrial cancer, along with the advice of doctors that a very aggressive treatment was necessary. Getting through 25 radiation sessions during a global pandemic along with extreme rounds of chemotherapy was extremely difficult, yet there were some powerful, transformative choices she made going through the process.

"It's a daunting thing to hear that you need to go through cancer treatment and with all the grueling things that come with it and all of a sudden your identity is going to change," she recalls. "The good news is that I made some amazing choices, and so the lessons that I learned coming out of cancer were my life is about making choices and I can make clear, positive choices or I can make choices that aren't going to work for me. But every moment of my life I have a choice and so I made some choices to form teams of experts that were going to help me figure out how to navigate this thing."

Displaying the traits of an exceptional leader by being very intentional in having a positive mindset and a bias to action was crucial in getting to the best possible outcome.

143

Even the most basic of things, including the approach to the treatment effects on her hair, came into play.

"I made choices to keep my brain nimble by going back and doing some really awesome programs on diversity and inclusion and an executive women's leadership program at Cornell while I was in chemotherapy. I made choices to say active every single day and I made choices that I was going to save my hair through an interesting process called cold capping," Conigliaro-Hubbard explains. "I actually save my hair through chemotherapy by cold capping and being super disciplined and making a lot of really clean, healthy choices."

Going through this scary experience was a motivator for Conigliaro-Hubbard to pursue other dreams, including authoring the book *Lessons In Life and Leadership* which captures the best from her interviews with 75 exceptional women leaders in her network. One of the consistent themes that emerged was how important the seeking of knowledge is to continuous growth.

"I couldn't help but be really astounded by how many women in different words had something very similar to say about the importance of continuing to learn. When we find ways to keep learning we expand our view of the world, we can be more creative, we can find more solutions to big challenges," she says. "Related to that, seek to expand boundaries and also lay boundaries down when they can bring value to the greater good. Too often we set boundaries and we turn them into these limiting realities for ourselves."

Conigliaro-Hubbard shared a great analogy from her

mother, Laura Conigliaro, in her book about building a hill of sand, grain by grain. For it to grow higher, it also has to grow wider.

"Those grains of sand or pieces of learning will enable you to come up with new and better insights and more creative solutions going beyond what you absolutely need to know It will make your job and your life richer and more rewarding. We expand our boundaries when we learn anything new that wasn't available to us before."

Figure 5.4 Hill of Sand

Leadership during times of great change is extremely hard, and doing it exceptionally well is even harder.

Vijay Velamoor was my HR partner at AirTouch and went on to senior HR and IT leadership roles with Harrah's and Asurion and is now an executive in residence/advisor to the business school at Georgetown University. Highly analytical with a global perspective shaped by early career experiences in India plus the Middle East, he feels effective change leadership is one of the biggest challenges companies face. Velamoor thinks of leadership during a changing environment falling into three basic categories: programmatic leadership, people leadership, and leader conduct.

When it comes to people leadership, engagement is key. He points to a McKinsey study showing when people feel a sense of ownership and are engaged, the success rate is more than 70%. Yet leaders often still need a reality check.

"There's a large gap between leaders' own belief that they are leading change effectively versus the belief of those that are affected by the change. A very significant fact in change research is the people variable which constitutes the difference between success and failure. Continued oversight in ensuring engagement and active participation of team members in managing changes remains a puzzle."

Velamoor also asserts a misplaced accusation is the oft-repeated claim by leaders that their efforts are blunted by others' resistance to change.

"This has become an alibi for change failure and suboptimal results," he says. "The question I think we should ask ourselves is why there is skepticism or outright rejection or resistance to change. The reasons are quite a few. First, change creates winners and losers. Winners are those who benefit from the change and since some of their friends or colleagues don't benefit from the change, the winners feel guilty. And guilt is sometimes experienced by the managers who have to give the bad news to those who will lose because of the change. Guilt can result in avoidance or blame."

Fortunately, there are plenty of examples of exceptional leaders who see reality for what it is, warts and all.

Matthew Schmidt is a multi-company Founder & CEO who is passionate about organizational health and paved his own unique road to exceptional leadership by learning some essential lessons in navigating some very challenging entrepreneurial waters in getting his companies Devada, and more recently Peoplelogic, off the ground and running. In the case of Devada, which resulted in a successful exit after 15 years, it was being able to handle the reality of being less than perfect.

"Along the way, we did a lot of things right. But we also did plenty of things wrong. One of the biggest learnings is that it's okay to make mistakes as you're growing your business. And the real trick is to avoid those fatal mistakes," Schmidt says. "You have to make mistakes, to learn and to grow, and to continue to iterate, and to course correct. And those very often will take a lot of different shapes."

Reflecting on the early years of getting through some big company challenges, Schmidt now has a much better appreciation for the inevitable ups and downs young businesses face and what separates truly exceptional leaders.

"Building a company is actually very much like riding a roller coaster, and doing it many, many, many times during the course of a single day. Being able to deal with those ups and downs and those mistakes and the failures and the successes and celebrating the wins," he says. "I will be the first to admit that I don't think I was always the best and acknowledging that these failures are opportunities for growth. Here at Peoplelogic, we're very focused on making sure people understand it's ok to make mistakes and to fail, as long as we grow from those and learn from those. But at the same time, we've got to be sure that we also celebrate the wins, regardless of the size of those wins. So, every day we make a point of surfacing the small wins for the team to celebrate and that we're all in this together, that we're rowing in the same direction."

Building internal momentum, synergy, and getting teams to rally around a company's key strategies are directly correlated to the clarity and frequency of leadership engagement. This is true for even the most established teams, let alone teams going through some significant people or structural changes.

Ken Myer is an accomplished executive with a track record of success in both for-profit and non-profit organizations including IBM, Active Voice, and the Washington Technology Industry Association. He currently serves as an advisor and interim executive for companies in transition and is a leadership and management lecturer at the University of Washington Foster School of Business. Myer is called upon by organizations to bring stability and transitional leadership where he has to quickly establish credibility and influence. He knows what it takes to be exceptional when inheriting a new team looking for a steady hand and support during a time of transition, and it isn't about doing all the talking and thinking you have all the answers already.

"I'm learning as time goes on the adage 'less is more' rings true at least for me," Myer says. "I'm learning that asking good questions is a real skill that you can't spend enough time working on as a leader, asking versus telling, you know, really listening and trying to figure out what for that person motivates them versus another person. Aligning people around a shared view of what you're trying to get done."

When coming in as an interim executive, sometimes in a stressful situation with as little as 48 hours' notice, there is not much time to plan anything elaborate for his first meeting with his new team. Instead, Myer takes a very straightforward approach.

"Not surprisingly, first impressions and building trust quickly is super key. We all have to be our authentic selves and I try to be very honest and clear and hopefully positive about why I am here. Why there is an interim leader in this situation? What do I know and what I don't know? What approach I'll take to work with them."

Drawing from his very diverse experiences in long-term and short-term interim executive assignments, one of the first questions Myer also asks his university business students is the age-old question of whether great leaders are born, or made. He sees it as a bit of both, but in reality, the question does not address the true dynamic of leadership *behavior*, which in Myer's view is approximately one-third influenced by genetic endowments and more than two-thirds influenced by life experience and motivation, and ability to develop.

"It isn't really the case that you are or are not a leader. You are either likely to be exhibiting positive leader behaviors or negative leader behaviors. So, it's not a set of traits, it's a state. It's about who you are as a human being in the act of trying to motivate and inspire or align or move a group of people that you're working with," he observes. "When you study how to become a better leader, you're really studying about how to become a better version of you."

Joli Mosier and **Jordan McCann** are co-founders at MosierMcCann, and for more than 20 years have provided strategic counsel to leaders seeking sustainable business growth through highly effective implementation. They also recognize that exceptional leadership is about continuously evolving, and welcoming continuous change as an incentive to drive better execution.

Exceptional leaders get their teams executing on strategy better by avoiding falling into a common trap of underestimating project complexity.

"One of the biggest obstacles we see is that companies just tend to oversimplify what is needed for implementation, so they don't recognize right up front what it's going to take and what they're going to need," Mosier says. We often hear things from clients if they've been struggling, 'how could it be that hard'? The reality is, an effective execution in a complex corporate environment requires a very specific set of highly developed skills like leadership, communications, planning, critical thinking, and much more."

There is no more painful waste in organizations than

when great strategies don't come to fruition in a timely fashion. McCann views the approach to talent acquisition as vital.

"Execution and implementation expertise is a category and a skill and thing all of its own," she says. "So, here's where we see most business leaders at whatever level where people go wrong when they think to go hire someone, whether it's even pulling someone internally or hiring from the outside you do not want to get fixated on functional and subject matter experience. But that is not the same person that has the execution experience typically."

I have always been fascinated by superior athletic performance, the intersection of physical training with mental preparation to deliver clutch performance in high-pressure moments. And there are some very relevant parallels to the business world.

My high school classmate **Kory Tarpenning** is a great case in point, excelling in one of the most highly technical track and field events (pole vault) through a disciplined approach to training that didn't just rely on natural physical traits of size or strength. He grew up in the track and field hotbed of Eugene, Oregon within a very athletic family with a father who was a championship-winning coach at the local community college. He was a four-time national champion and represented the United States in the 1988 and 1992 Olympics, finishing 10th and 4th, respectively.

After retiring from competitive track and field, Tarpenning began a successful entrepreneurial career, opening the first Starbucks location in Monaco and bringing Nike-branded retail stores to multiple locations in France and Monaco. He sees the connection between his athletic and business success comes down to how he approaches preparation, offering an interesting analogy from his school days.

"I can say 90% of success is preparation and a small bit of luck that might pop in there every now and again, but what people can really relate to is if you are preparing yourself for an exam that's coming up. And sometimes you go in and you walk out and say 'wow, that was a really easy test' or if you're not prepared you come out and say that's a really hard test," he says. "I looked at it the same way in sports where I was preparing, I was training really hard and if I was prepared well, I'd go to competition, that was my exam, that was my test. The same thing in business, if you plan your business well and you are prepared for all the different elements, usually you can have pretty good success."

Hockey legend Wayne Gretzky once famously observed that you miss 100% of the shots you *don't* take. Tarpenning agrees that exceptional leadership means *going for it,* setting aside internal fear of failure in the persistent pursuit of your goals.

"I failed many, many times but at the same time I was persistent to go back and try again, being patient enough to that there's a developmental process," he reflects. "You can't expect to be successful in business overnight. I know there is a lot of immediacy to the current generation. But I think you still need to look at the long-term approach, plan for the long term, and work toward the long term. The day I opened Starbucks in Monaco, people just saw suddenly the arrival. But what most people don't know is I was working on that for five years before it opened its' doors."

TAKEAWAYS CHECKLIST:

☑ Building your leadership foundation around respect for people is made stronger by focusing on a triad of empowerment, transparency, and accountability

☑ Advocate for increasing emotional intelligence across all levels in your organization to create greater connections and better business results

☑ Exceptional leadership is not a trait, it is a state that is a reflection of your behaviors and part of a process that is all about becoming a better version of you

6

Optimism

---

op·ti·mism - *hopefulness and confidence about the future*

Attitude is everything in leadership. Just as a leader's pessimistic perspective often becomes a self-fulfilling prophecy and sucks the life out of a team, optimism is contagious and lifts the spirit—and performance—of teams to new levels. Being optimistic is a deliberate choice that each of us has full control over making. Looking at a glass of water, is it half-empty...or half-full? My experience has been that choosing to be hopeful and confident about the future while visualizing positive outcomes as a leader creates an energizing environment for others that helps motivate them to do their best work.

The uncertainty and strife in our world today make it hard to maintain an optimistic perspective. With everything from the global COVID pandemic, unstable financial markets, inflation, escalating gun violence, wars and more being covered around the clock in real-time by the mass media and documented through social media, there are plenty of reasons to be pessimistic. But through it all, there *are* reasons for being optimistic about the future as well.

Rob Grady, who has achieved entrepreneurial success in growing a new business at Amazon as the General Manager of the Amazon Freight Partner program, sees a bright future through the lens of the next generation of leaders he works with in mentoring students in both the University of Washington Foster School of Business and Athletic Department.

"They're very smart and ambitious, but also balanced... they have a highly nuanced view of the world...looking through the lens of what's important and valuable to them makes me very optimistic," he says. 'They're thoughtful with their questions, they are deeper and more insightful than what I asked when I was at the same place in my career development...it gives me great hope for the future. In particular, there are so many opportunities to re-think and re-create industries that we haven't even thought of yet, and ways to re-create public services like education as well. With the right tools and opportunities, the next generation is set up to succeed, which makes me optimistic for the future."

Author, coach, and motivational speaker **Donnie Boivin** has gone from serving honorably in the U.S. Marine Corp to spending more than two decades mastering sales and marketing. The Founder and CEO of the Success Champion family of companies remain optimistic about the unprecedented entrepreneurial opportunities that exist today. With broader access to emerging technology, it's no wonder he rallies behind the phrase "It's time to go big."

"As a society as a whole, we are in the greatest time. Growing up as a kid I didn't know you could start your own company," he reflects. "You know I wasn't the entrepreneur kid that had the lemonade stands or was a top salesman of boy scout cookies or anything like that, so this idea that with nothing more than a phone you can transform and change your life and grow and make something big I mean I'm completely blown away like this whole NFT space right now and what's going on there I think that's going to completely change the world and I think this is as big as the internet happening and like when the internet first came in. I think our whole world of currency and everything's going to shift to that marketplace and that excites me because the only way to currently learn that stuff is you got to go out and be amongst it and be around the people that are doing and building and creating. Admittedly I'm still learning all this stuff and I'm completely overwhelmed by the massive amount of knowledge in the NFT space and cryptocurrencies, and those things is completely overwhelming but I'm embracing that learning process and what it takes to build in that space."

What his optimism boils down to is a truly global "leveling of the playing field" when it comes to opportunity and the ability to achieve financial success.

"It's the most fantastic time to live because now you take success and you literally give it to the blue-collar, up-and-coming people. You give it to the third-world countries, as long as somebody has a cell phone they can completely transform and change their life. People are too hung up on world news and society and I think once they realize that all that stuff doesn't matter, they're going to going to find a cool freedom by building their own world that impacts others."

Michael Litt has impacted many as the co-founder and CEO of the online video platform Vidyard. To him, personal freedom in how and where we work is transformational by making humans more productive and able to pursue everything that helps them be all they can be.

"The flexibility of working from a location of your desire whether that is your home whether that is somewhere in Costa Rica, or a beach is a very powerful thing for people as it relates to the integration of both work and life," he says. "The three hours of commuting per day that many people were subject to pre-pandemic, I hope they are able to break away from because that's three hours that could be spent with your family, that could be spent educating yourself on a topic, that could be spent on a side hustle, that could be spent fulfilling a dream. On the other side of all this humanity will have adapted the use of technology in the concept of work and will have shed some of the expectations of work-life culture that existed prior to the pandemic that were a byproduct of the pre-war era and I think that is a good thing and I think that is a very positive thing for the benefit of humanity in general."

The freedom for market disruptors who believe in a people-first culture to transform customer experiences is another reason to be optimistic.

In the case of the mature $100+ billion global elevator industry, dominated by just a handful of large companies, **Ashleigh Wilson** has brought a fresh, customer-focused, and people-focused perspective to Audimate, the company she founded and where she serves as CEO.

Raised in a family of elevator operators, inspectors, and business managers, she is redefining the customer experience for those seeking to optimize their elevator maintenance service contracts. To Wilson, a bright future is all about the next generation who she feels a special connection with and is empowered to access business knowledge in an entirely different way.

"Accessibility to information makes me optimistic. I'm in my thirties so the fact that I'm like kids these days already makes me chuckle," she says. "But watching the generation of teenagers right now that consume information and are making sure that subjects are so accessible to everybody is extremely inspiring to me and there's no reason that we don't understand legal documents or that we don't understand contracts we're signing and things of that nature because it is possible to make all information accessible and kind of blowing up and destroying the gatekeeping of knowledge is something that I'm just in awe of and want to be a part of."

Ultimately, it's about having access to information that ensures we make intelligent decisions in our journey to a better life.

"Everybody has the right to understand the systems and the processes and the contracts that we have to sign to just live. Leases and credit cards and all of these different things, we sign these documents and many of us don't know. That's just a small part of it, but the direction that I'm heading is everybody has the right to understand what we have to do and the things that we have to agree to in living a safe and happy life."

Sales is one of the most dynamic corporate functions at the intersection of people, processes, and results, where goals are the most tangible and measured in precise increments. Despite the gravitational pull of legacy approaches to prospecting and managing sales relationships in a dynamically changing marketplace, there are optimistic signs companies are recognizing the need to adapt or suffer dire consequences.

John Flannery, the founder of Flannery Sales Systems, works with companies around the world to optimize their sales processes. Having worked closely with him on major sales and marketing process evolution when I was in the fitness industry several years back, I also saw up close how critical the ability—and willingness—to adapt is too consistent performance improvement when the behaviors of your buyers are changing.

"The status quo is always the biggest obstacle to redefine or implement a sales process," he says. "More than ten years ago buying changed radically at the onset of the great recession. Our customers who are successful understand the need to adapt and change and making sure their sellers are adept at all of the skills needed to be successful in field, or inside sales, or other customer-facing roles. It's continuous improvement."

Figure 6.1 Sales Process

WWW.ANDERTOONS.COM

"We started playing Horse, then switched to Bird, then Cow, then Ox, and now we're just playing Z."

Mike Wills, CEO of Apex Order Pickup Solutions, which is transforming the supply chain experience for retail, food service, and restaurant customers, has an impressive sales leadership background for major companies including Zebra Technologies, Intermec, and Motorola. For him, optimism starts with attitude.

"It is a choice, right? It's a natural choice for me. I'd rather be optimistic than pessimistic. Frankly, the markets in general. People aspire, you know the human nature is to aspire to better myself, my surroundings, my life, and my community in general. That description doesn't fit everybody but in general, I still believe in the broad majority of people think that way wake up every day that way," he reflects. "Because of that, our collective careers in technology that continue to use the speed and the quantity of accessible action-based data for decision making is an exciting way to do it, because that there's a direct corollary to improving people's lives when you're making better decisions."

Wills sees the last few challenging years with a global health crisis reaffirming his confidence in the human spirit.

"This pandemic was it was highly personal. We all have somebody that we know or somebodies that we know that we're affected by it. But we also saw the full demonstration the accomplishments made by our human side of our organization looking to offset the downside and the disastrous effects of this virus on a global basis. Coming together and in an unprecedented manner to get a vaccine together and put this behind us."

"Don't miss an opportunity to make a personal connection with your team. And what I mean by that specifically is taking an interest in what's going on in their lives and actually remembering it and bumping into them a week later or two weeks or three weeks later and inquiring about that," he suggests.

This is a classic example where the accumulation of small, meaningful gestures pays off in a big way.

"It may be the smallest little anecdotal piece of information they shared with you that can unlock unbelievable retention with members in your team and basically what they're hearing is 'hey my leadership heard me. They took a vested interest and asked me genuinely what was going on I shared something with them and trust number one, it didn't go the wrong way and that it wasn't a negative outcome. It was a very positive outcome and they care about me as an individual.'"

Wills' optimism is fueled by his confidence in the foundation of healthy organizations, and the driver for results comes from teams—not just senior leadership.

"While leaders get so tasked to delivering results and delivering a return to our shareholders and stakeholders in general, it's our team that does it...don't ever forget that!"

There is nothing more breathtaking than seeing entire teams, even entire organizations, rally together in challenging times behind a collective spirit of optimism to achieve outcomes that seem out of reach initially. It's common for communities to come together in times of crisis, be it from natural disasters, horrendous criminal acts like mass shootings, or financial crises.

I lead a very talented marketing team at Committee for Children, a non-profit that for more than 40 years has championed the safety and well-being of kids along with developing a wide range of leading social-emotional learning (SEL) programs positively impacting educational staff and student experiences around the world. The global COVID pandemic created huge disruption in the education market, and revenue to programs to providers like Committee for Children, as districts and schools had to figure out quickly new models for supporting students virtually or even hybrid. The seismic shift in priorities and focus in a very short period of time raised a lot of questions and uncertainty about what the near-term future would have in store. It meant my non-profit had to quickly pivot to better serve its clients—or risk being branded as tone-deaf and not relevant.

For twelve months in a macro-environment of tremendous stress and uncertainty, I was blessed to contribute to something remarkable, powered by a continuous stream of optimistic staff communications from senior leadership plus the formation of new cross-functional tiger teams to hyper-accelerate the development of new program and communication supports for key existing clients. Barely two years removed from the initial onset of pandemic chaos, the organization achieved unprecedented levels of program enhancement and new program launches, along with record revenue attainment and program reach in support of its mission.

Sometimes moments of levity in the face of big problems can help us get through the toughest times. In the spirit of keeping my team motivated, I started peppering an interesting phrase into my 1:1 conversations with one of my most senior direct reports. We were both amazed at the unprecedented change taking place in our personal and business lives, with so many ups and downs and reasons to stress and lose our optimism. Our own Pacific Northwest weather teaches a lesson. Gray skies and raindrops only last so long. At some point clouds clear. When discussing some of the finer "lowlights" of the week, I would blurt out "I think I can see the sun coming out" and that would get us laughing. It helped.

Resilience matters. There's a famous saying by Robert

H. Schuller that "tough times never last, but tough people do!" Attitude and outlook in times of challenge are *everything*, it can be the difference between hopeless resignation or an unplanned epiphany that results in unimaginable benefits. And when life delivers the ultimate curveball, it may also be the catalyst for a true life transformation.

Case in point: **Marthin DeBeer**.

Transitioning from spending 20 years building high-growth, billion-dollar-plus businesses at Cisco, he founded and now serves as CEO of his own company BrightPlan to drive greater employee wellness through the development of comprehensive, personalized financial plans. The genesis for his latest entrepreneurial success did not start in prosperity, as the inspiration for BrightPlan was borne out of a personal, family crisis. Supporting his wife's recovery from an unexpected, severe illness during a sabbatical required a shift in his priorities and a re-evaluation of what was truly important to him. It also forced him to reexamine his financial plan more deeply and he made some important discoveries.

"Wealth and finances are very closely related. Money is everyone's problem but we don't even teach our kids how to use a credit card in high school so people often get well educated they work really hard and then they make very poor financial decisions or they get very poor advice. And you know the result is very predictable," he says.

"I had that time and started to think about how often people that have financial challenges become sick or people that are experiencing health challenges, it places a big financial burden on them, financial health and physical health are inextricably tied together and the one affects the other in a profound way. I had time to look deeper into my own situation. I thought I was a smart guy and I thought I had life figured out and I was doing really well at a Fortune 500 company. As I started asking much tougher questions and probing questions of my advisors at a private bank, it became clear to me that I did not have a rock-solid plan in place and in fact. That I wasn't well positioned for retirement one day and that the advice I've been receiving was really not in my best interest. I was in very illiquid securities that had big fees associated with it and I didn't even understand that. So that really hit home for me because I realized that if I didn't see that coming and I didn't understand exactly where I was, and I'm a fairly savvy financial business person, then there must be millions of people that are in the same boat."

Applying optimism and your positive energy to tackling a very real problem that deeply affects you on a personal level is indeed a powerful thing. It can be the difference between pursuing business goals versus pursuing a *life* purpose. That was certainly true for DeBeer.

"I would have loved to apply my skillset to do something with real purpose in the medical field based on what my wife lived through but that's not my area of expertise," he reflects. "But I know that you know software can crunch numbers and that financial wellness is a solvable problem with the software. And so that is what set the wheels in motion for me. I really want to pursue this much greater purpose of helping none of the people live better lives, happier and better lives. That's really what led me to start BrightPlan."

Figure 6.2 Career Transition

Paul Green, the owner of MSP Marketing Edge and host of the MSP Marketing podcast, is another example of bringing passion and optimism into a major career change. Formerly an accomplished broadcast host in the UK, he now helps Managed Service Providers (MSPs) successfully market and grow their businesses. He is excited about the continuous evolution of humanity.

"What makes me optimistic is our adaptability. I genuinely believe in the ingenuity of humans and I believe in our ability to make incredible connections and to be led by incredible people and I don't mean politicians. You know Elon Musk's driving thing is not to be rich. He is the world's richest man but what's driving him is making a backup of the human species," Green says. "He wants to put people on Mars not because it'll be fun to be on Mars. But because it's the next step in backing up the human species. So, if the planet just does happen to go it's okay, we've got people backed up to another planet and you know if he's able to achieve that in his lifetime, what an amazing thing."

Working in space defined by delivering technology-based solutions, Green is energized by the seemingly limitless possibilities that technology brings.

"In the last twenty to thirty years, we seem to have moved to a point now where you can have any idea and there are a lot of people very open to it. We're very open to new things. Our technology is moving forward at an extraordinary pace. You are limited in your technology and your marketing more or less by your ideas more than you are by the technology," he says. "Although I think these are very dangerous times ahead and I wouldn't want to be my daughter's daughter's daughter because I think that's going to be really scary for that generation, at the same time I think we are at a point where we should be able to fix this and be positive about the future."

From Green's perspective, the next generation is benefiting tremendously from advanced technology and brings new freedom to think more boldly.

"In terms of business, I'm optimistic because change creates opportunity and we're going to see more and more and more change. You know the baby boomers, we're all retiring right now that's creating massive change. It's happening all across the world. As long as humans can be free to think in big ways and take big action, that gives me huge optimism and it's wonderful," he says. "I am a sole parent. Just me and my daughter. It's actually lovely to sit and watch her grow up. It's wonderful to watch someone growing up in this world where you know she has got a phone that's at her side for ten hours a day. As much as I'm not a big fan of Tiktok. I am a big fan of what technology is allowing her to do. When I was growing up, you had to go to a library and look it up in an encyclopedia and now she just asks Alexa. You know she doesn't she doesn't have to even look it up on a device and you've got to say to yourself: what are these guys going to be doing in thirty years' time?"

Ross Daniels, CMO at customer experience solution provider Calabrio, is another former Cisco colleague of mine. Having served in several product marketing and channel marketing leadership roles, his focus as a newer member of the C-suite is enabling his teams in solving complex problems for his customers to help them deliver more outstanding customer experiences. Daniels sees contact centers, as the hub of customer interactions, having stayed constant in many ways over the years, but he is very optimistic about the future.

"What excites me is the way they've changed," he says. "The notion that customer experience really does matter. It matters to companies' bottom lines; it matters in terms of customer retention. You have Chief Customer Officers actually a thing, leading companies now, it is not a novelty like it was a few years ago. These officers are tracking the customer journey in all elements. It can lead into marketing. From a technology standpoint, the move to the cloud allows for so more flexibility, much more omnichannel or digital service tools. It's a much richer set of data we now have access to and can provide insights on, visualizing them for customer service operators so they can do better, so they can improve their net promoter score or customer effort. We give them that view that they need to be able to make changes to improve."

To Daniels, an important part of a bright future for continuously improving customer solutions is how more intensely competitive markets are putting an even greater premium on understanding customer needs. It's at the cornerstone of his advice for business leaders.

"Pay attention to the customer, at the expense of everything else. It's the lifeblood of your business. Don't think of the contact center as a cost, it is an investment in your customers and give the people running them their due respect and the tools they need to be effective," he advises. "Go listen to some of these customer calls, understand what their problems are."

Firaas Rashid is also very passionate about customer experience. With an entrepreneur's spirit, he was a fast riser at Credit Suisse and App Dynamics. Amid the pandemic, he founded Hook in 2020, a predictive data platform that empowers customer success teams by providing accurate revenue predictions and intelligent, actionable insights to secure renewals in a subscription business. He has raised multi-millions of dollars in funding from some of the most prestigious investors and company founders in Europe. His excitement for the future is all about the unlimited opportunities for young companies in the new economy.

"My personal excitement is we're based in London and I remember when I first went to San Francisco ten years ago I was having breakfast in the hotel and there was a guy sitting next to me that was pitching a VC and I remember thinking at the time, how amazing it was to be in this world in San Francisco where all this was the norm. I've been obsessed with it since I was young as I've always wanted to do entrepreneurial things and I think the amazing thing that I've seen in the last three years is that has become also the norm in London and in Europe so you've seen this huge growth of investment in Europe you've seen amazing startups and unicorns. That's got a cyclical effect because people come out of those companies and start to drive their own startups. Most recently I've met founders in my gym changing room, I've met them in bars, I've had lunch outside a cafe and there's been VCs talking about driving an increase in the number of LPs they've got. And so, I'm really excited about the opportunity London's got and Europe has got as we kind of start to become this huge tech hub in the world."

Rashid sees a bright, customer-focused future being largely shaped by how well businesses take advantage of the huge amounts of customer data they will have at their fingertips.

"You've got to focus on maximizing your outcomes from your existing customers. Business leaders tend to deprioritize that. In order to do that you need to figure out how you can use data to do it. People use loads of data in the sales process and it can be very predictable to run a sales machine. Companies tend to be very bad at using data in the post-sales process but the problem is

171

that makes your operation inefficient because you end up with a very expensive route to recovering customers. Focus on data make sure that you're focused on maximizing your existing customers and find what the leading indicators are for making that happen."

The ongoing survival of true capitalism is enough to get **Kristin Zhivago**, President of Zhivago Partners, excited. For decades she has been helping companies develop winning marketing and revenue strategies and is a passionate believer in the positive impact of a free enterprise system.

"I do believe in capitalism, I think that it works. It's always worked. It's not the prettiest, cleanest system in the world but there is no such thing as a perfect system. But it's better than the opposite," she says. "Letting the customer lead the way and having people try to meet those customer needs and get paid for it, It's pretty good. I'm always optimistic on that level. I'm a serial entrepreneur, there's a lot of hope there. It goes back to that whole love idea where you're taking care of other people through your products and services and providing a happy place for people to work, I mean that's a pretty good contribution to society. I'm very happy with being a person who does that so that makes me optimistic."

Zhivago points to a very vivid example from one very well-known global online retailer that has continuously innovated to create unique, positive customer experiences.

"Something that people don't really realize right now, but the thing that is working for any type of product or service is going above and beyond so you don't just answer their question about the measurement of the system that they're buying, You know this physical object and how big is it. You actually show close-up pictures, and you do a 360 view and you show reviews and you know Amazon's really set the bar on all of that stuff and it's amazing to me how many companies have not copied what they're doing because they're very good at making it easy for you to spend money at Amazon," she says.

"And they do it by just keep adding value to keep answering questions even letting customers answer other customers' questions and do reviews and stuff like that. It's just been amazing. You know that's why Jeff Bezos is a billionaire, and he's also a billionaire because he was a process company from the start. It didn't matter he was selling books and when he came out I thought to myself, 'Well this isn't a product or service company. It's a process company.' So they just applied that to every product in the universe. I find that the companies that keep thinking 'how can I give more value? How can I make it easier for them to make a decision to learn about this? What can I do to just make it easier for the person?' Those are the companies that are succeeding right now."

Figure 6.3 Customer Satisfaction

Sarah Nicastro is passionate about how companies accel at delivering outstanding customer service in the field. A Future of Field Service evangelist and having formerly served more than a decade as an Editor In Chief for *Field Technologies* magazine, she works closely with services organizations to better utilize technology in strategically improving their business.

"One of the things that that I feel most optimistic about and most excited about is all of the potential that exists in service. We're sort of at a point where the things that that I. started covering when I entered this space are all kind of coming to fruition and becoming real opportunity and real value for organizations."

As excited as she is about where service delivery is today, Nicastro sees even more potential being realized in the years ahead as an intensely competitive marketplace pushes customer focus to the forefront of strategic priorities.

"There are a lot of exciting things to come. There is a lot of potential in service yet to be realized and that's really exciting and I'm thrilled to be able to play a role in helping organizations understand that potential and connecting them with one another to help work toward that potential," she says. "You can't be customer-centric without customer intimacy. There's no shortcut to that. Make sure you recognize the connection between employee engagement and customer satisfaction. Over the past few years, as organizations have worked toward the potential and focused a lot on the customer experience, we've maybe overlooked a bit the connection of how imperative our employees are in executing on that customer experience. We need to make sure that we have a good culture, that we have employees who feel valued who are engaged who enjoy what they do. Ultimately that is what is going to help us deliver that positive experience and you know maintain those relationships over the long term."

While an advocate for the impact of technology, Nicastro is careful to not overlook the importance of culture and the people inside it.

"In a lot of years of having all of these conversations, it's almost always the people part that either has the biggest impact or causes the biggest problems depending on how you look at it right? It's typically the hardest to get right," she says. "There's so much development and sophistication in technology and there's a lot of power there and a lot of room to expand and increase capabilities and evolve service delivery but it doesn't work if you don't get the people part right, both on the customer side and the employee side."

We live in a world dominated by online media, a world of real-time information capture with an estimated 1.5 trillion online searches performed every year. For **Eli Schwartz**, a Search Engine Optimization (SEO) expert who has consulted with some of the internet's top brands for more than a decade and helped fuel growth at Survey Monkey in leading their early SEO efforts, the power of global information access via an ever-increasing volume of online searches is a big reason to be optimistic.

"There are a lot of reasons to be optimistic about the world, I think we're certainly seeing a decline in globalization and a decline in personal relationships. I like to see people using technology and searching more and more. I think that SEO in search has become incredibly helpful to people, so much so, that we want to put devices in our houses that allow us to search more. Assistant devices and our phones are even more useful on than before. And Amazon is currently the only one with glasses and I think that Google is going to have glasses and Facebook's going to have glasses and everyone's going to have glasses where you can do searches and really conduct and interact with technology more and I think that SEO is so helpful and required for this kind of thing."

Schwartz explains at its' core, SEO is a very simple concept.

"All you're doing is optimizing your ability to show up

on search. There's no magic sauce there and if you don't optimize yourself just for search, you're just leaving this to luck. So as people do more and more searches, there are more opportunities for companies to be found and more opportunities for products to be found," he says. "It's not about 'I just need to be visible in the single keyword I'm obsessed with' it's 'I need to be visible for the users that are looking for me when they're looking for me and there's more opportunities for them to look for us as the technology goes into more places'. We'll have a massive backlash against 'do we need a technology break?' but we're not there yet. As much as people say we're on our phones too much, no one is saying 'I'm locking my phone up' and there's not a huge movement to lock up phones just yet."

Schwartz recommends developing unique strategies based on deep customer and user understanding to achieve a competitive advantage in his optimistic future.

"Really focus on long-term growth. I don't care about competitors when it comes to SEO, I think if all you do is copy your competitors, you will always be behind them. Motley Fool produces 120 pieces of financial content per day. If someone decides they want to go into the financial content space, they need to catch up to 120 pieces of content per day. Not only that they need to catch up to ten years of 120 pieces of content per day," to outpace Motley Fool today to do that," he observes. "But if you have an interesting thing to offer the financial space, find your angle, don't copy. Don't copy Robin Hood, don't copy Yahoo Finance. I think there's so many things you can do if you just get creative. Talk to your customers, and understand what they're looking for if you're a venture-funded business. There's a reason that the venture capitalists and investors were inspired to give you the money and that's what you should build strategies and SEO strategies around, not copying others but really understanding your users and building for users and thinking about what are my users going to want for me in 2025? What can I build for them and not think about 'what do my users need for me today, I'll build for them today' because if it's that easy anyone can do it."

Karthik Suresh is co-founder of Ignition, a collaborative hub to manage more effective go-to-market (GTM) processes end-to-end to help Product Marketing and Product teams create more internal alignment on launch plans, assets, and execution. Even amid market uncertainty, he is very optimistic about the fast pace of innovation.

"What keeps me optimistic, what makes me get me up every day is literally the pace of innovation that's happening. In this industry, you know whether you look at self-driving cars or the machine learning and ai in general, even on the medical side of things, the genetics in our vaccines, The covid vaccine was a new technology," he says.

Suresh is especially in awe of the pace of change in the 21st century, even in mature industries that traditionally have been much slower to transform.

"We see all of these crypto and Web3 innovations which hopefully are going to make our financial systems better. If there's one thing which can save us from ourselves, that's technology. What's even more interesting is the pace of change in technology is accelerating," he observes. "Ten years ago, talking about an electric car was like 'hey that's probably like 2050' and now we not just have Tesla but every single traditional car company like GM and Ford and BMW and Mercury. Everyone is thinking electric cars. The next set of innovation is going to be automation, because a lot of the mundane jobs, people are getting more and more skilled. So, then we need like robots to help do all the of them like our mundane jobs so there is a ton of innovation continuing to happen, irrespective of the market conditions and irrespective of what else is happening in the world."

Jamison West, a serial entrepreneur who built and sold his own businesses and helps others successfully grow their businesses as a coach with ConnectStrat, is also very optimistic about how technology will shape the future.

"I'm such a natural optimist that just about everything I'm always looking forward and seeing an opportunity for me right now," he says. "It's just the speed of technology, the breaking down of barriers, even the acceleration that happened through the pandemic. I love to travel and I'm still traveling a tremendous amount and at the end of the day, it's significantly multiplied the number of people I can touch and connect with through technology. Things I can accomplish in moments, that used to take hours. I can't even imagine what this has will look like 10 years from now and it just gets me excited. I talk about Elon Musk because I'm a bit of a fan, I drive it I drive a Tesla, and it drives me across town, and like I didn't think that would happen ten years ago and here it is happening and it's just pretty stunning. So, I'm excited always about technology driving us forward."

To benefit fully from this technology-driven future, West advises business leaders to build clarity in their long-term vision—and don't be afraid to seek help from others. It can literally mean the difference between achieving your long-term goals or failing from the start.

"Unless you feel that you have balance in your business, a clear vision for where you want to go, clarity on how you're going to differentiate over the next few years, surrounded by strong operators, go talk to people, get help. I realized at the beginning of my journey I was really kind of alone in my business as the Leader. Not only through coaching and consulting but peer groups, there's also a peer group in my MSP industry that I started back in the day. There are so many people that you can lean into. You don't need to reinvent the wheel. Leaders who are wanting to move and grow, they need to realize that there's resources outside their four walls that can help get them there and that those resources are not only available for them, but for other leaders and potential leaders on their team. Every now and then I'll see organizations that are just so contained and not connecting with the resources outside their walls and they're just limiting themselves. There's so much more you can do and it's not just the coaching and kind of work I do. There's so much out there. Even coaches need coaches to be able to get outside your head and communicate outside of your day-to-day just exposes you to new ideas and opportunities and options and I think everybody needs that. Personally, and professionally there's moments, whether it's a confidante or a friend, you have to be able to get out of your head. In the business world, sometimes that's hard to do with your family and friends they may not be in that world. So, getting out and finding somebody who can speak that language and understand what you're going through can be very, very helpful."

TAKEAWAYS CHECKLIST:

☑ Optimism is a cornerstone for effective, impactful leadership and is a very personal, deliberate choice

☑ Amazing technology advances that are transforming the customer experience are one of the biggest reasons to be optimistic about the future

☑ People, even more than process and technology, will continue to be the foundation of an optimistic future

A WARM SUMMER

The Impact Makers have spoken. The voices of leadership in this book echo perspectives associated with successful outcomes achieved around the world.

Being intentional about creating a strong culture of innovation, embracing diversity, nurturing healthy trusted relationships, intelligently using data, committing to excellence in the practice of leadership and maintaining an optimistic outlook is the foundation of making a meaningful, positive impact every day.

Life is a series of choices: where to live, where to work, where to play, and most importantly, *what kind of life do I want to lead?*

Leaders of people, teams, and organizations make fundamental choices every day that ultimately shape their legacy. As a leader, you ask yourself deeply personal questions that define your own leadership brand.

Should I be *inspiring* or *intimidating*?

Should I be *empowering* or *controlling*?

Should I be *motivating* or *managing*?

Should I be *elevating* or *deflating*?

Should I be *authentic* or *calculating*?

Embracing servant leadership is an amazing journey that will generate countless uplifting moments as you watch your teams accomplish things you may never have thought possible. When you deliberately shift your universe from revolving solely around *you* to what you can fully enable in *others*, perspectives change...for the better. The ripple effect of confident, engaged leadership exponentially scales in delivering better results back to the organization, and a feeling of accomplishment like no other.

As an author, educator and presidential advisor Booker T. Washington exclaimed more than a century ago, "if you want to lift yourself up, lift up someone else."

Impactful leadership is about bringing true passion into everything you do. A mindset of merely going through the motions, or just checking the boxes, is more transparent—and contagious—to others than you think. It's the difference between being a professional manager who is obsessed with accumulating self-credits and climbing the ranks versus being a leader who cares at a deeper emotional level about removing barriers and developing the people closest to them. Your emotional commitment will be a sustainable energy source over time.

In their book *The Leadership Challenge*, James Kouze and Barry Posner point out that "of all the things that sustain a leader over time, love is the most lasting. The best-kept secret of successful leaders is love: staying in love with leading, with the people who do the work, with what their organizations produce, and with those who honor the organization by using its work."

How great would it be to wake up every day and *love* all facets of what you do for a living? To be a dynamic force in the growth and well-being of others...and the communities they serve? The most gratifying and meaningful feedback I've received from people I've led over the years has never included their gratitude for having been *managed* well. The outpouring of thanks is typically about me having their backs, of supporting their development and having *enabled* them to reach their full potential. The kind of leadership my young marketing manager self-craved so long ago in a cold winter.

And so, for each of us as time marches on, our life experiences offer the precious gift of learning to shape decisions that define our leadership impact. As immortalized in the Indiana Jones film trilogy, "choose wisely."

Choose to be the person you *want* to be.

To be the leader you *can* be.

To be the Impact Maker you *deserve* to be.

INDEX

A

Accardi, Michelle, 83, 139–40
Account Based Marketing (ABM), 45–46
Alliance for Board Diversity (ABD), 78
Amazon, 19, 78, 156, 173, 176
Apple brand, 45
Arise Virtual Solutions, 20
Aruba Networks, 137
AST computers, 70
Asurion, 145
AWS, 18

B

Balanced Scorecard, 3
Batchery, 11
Big, Hairy, and Audacious Goals (BHAGs), 100
BILLY Footwear, 10
Bisnette, Bridget, 70–72, 83
Bissani, Karen, 83, 94
Bk97 Digital, 1
Blackmer, Laura, 33–36, 83
Blockbuster, 95
BMW, 179
board diversification, 81–82
Boivin, Donnie, 83, 156

organization dynamics, 73
OSG, 108
outlook, 53, 165, 183
ownership, 118, 131, 146

P

pandemic, global, xii, 20, 28, 31, 40, 113, 142–43, 155, 163
Pariveda, 141
Parkin, Tim, 87, 106–7
partnering, 7, 13, 18–19, 23–24, 27, 40–41, 43–45, 52–54, 68, 70–71, 91, 94
partnerships, 19, 23, 41, 43–44
Pattison, Mark, 49–50, 87
Peoplelogic, 147–48
performance, 15, 28, 32, 96, 122–23, 126, 130–31, 133–35, 137, 142, 151, 155, 160
personalization, 45, 93, 120, 123, 165
perspectives, diverse, 56, 60, 64–65, 77, 79, 91
Pinnaca, 110
Plantronics, 46
Polycom, 46
Prentice, Steve, 87, 111–12
Price, Billy, 10–11, 87
Proctor, Don, 1–2, 87
productivity, 16, 25, 135
product launches, 5–6, 137
product marketing, vii, 5, 9, 17, 45, 63, 75, 91, 103–4, 169, 178
prospects, 6, 27, 44–45, 91–92, 107–8, 117, 119–20

Q
Qualtrics, 36

R
Rashid, Firaas, 87, 170–71
Reasner, Steve, 87, 141
recruiting, v, x, 8, 15–16, 21–22, 52, 57–59, 64, 66, 77
repetition, 30, 48, 99, 123
resilience, 13, 164
resilient, 13–14, 42, 142, 164
Richardson Howell, Sharon, 87
Ridge, Nancy, 40, 88
Ridge Innovative, 40
risks, 16, 19, 132
Robinson, Kathryn, 8, 88
Roudebush, Megan, 29–31, 88

S
Sawkins, Clive, 88, 110–11
Schmidt, Matthew, 88, 147
Schwartz, Eli, 88, 176–77
Scott, Karyn, 58, 88
security, 16, 45, 56, 110–11, 113–14, 166
SEL (social-emotional learning), 163
SEO (Search Engine Optimization), 44, 176–78
service delivery, 174, 176
Shafer, Peter, 88, 121–22
Shroyer, Jonathan, 20–23, 88
silos, 4, 26, 114, 118
SMALIK Enterprises, 38
Smith, Keri, 32, 88

Made in the USA
Columbia, SC
12 October 2022